Presented to

_____

By

_____

On the Occasion of

_____

Date

_____

THANK YOU, LORD

Encouragement from
Anita Donihue

BARBOUR
PUBLISHING

© 2006 by Anita Corrine Donihue

Compiled by Erin Marshall

ISBN 1-59789-414-1

Published by Barbour Publishing, Inc., P.O. Box 719, Uhrichsville, Ohio 44683, www.barbourbooks.com

Our mission is to publish and distribute inspirational products offering exceptional value and biblical encouragement to the masses.

Member of the
Evangelical Christian
Publishers Association

Printed in the United States of America.
5 4 3 2 1

Contents

Introduction 7

Chapter 1: Thank You for Loving Me 9

Chapter 2: Thank You for Saving Me. 23

Chapter 3: Thank You for Blessing Me. 35

Chapter 4: Thank You for Being Faithful 49

Chapter 5: Thank You for Forgiveness 63

Chapter 6: Thank You for Family and Friends .77

Chapter 7: Thank You for Your Church 92

Chapter 8: Thank You for Growing Me 104

Chapter 9: Thank You for Guiding Me 118

Chapter 10: Thank You for Trials 132

Chapter 11: Thank You for Being Near 144

Chapter 12: Thank You for Prayer 158

Chapter 13: Thank You for Comforting Me. . .172

Chapter 14: Thank You for Healing Me. 184

Chapter 15: Thank You for Rest. 198

Chapter 16: Thank You for the Future 210

INTRODUCTION

In 1996, author Anita Corrine Donihue assembled a proposal for a book she called *Great Things Happen When I'm on My Knees*. A pastor's wife and public school educator from Washington State, Anita also dreamed of writing. Little did she know that this small book of meditations, published under the shortened title of *When I'm on My Knees*, would begin a series of six books that would sell well in excess of one million copies.

Hundreds of thousands of women responded to the warm, inviting, heartfelt thoughts of *When I'm on My Knees*. Over the next few years, five new titles followed: *When I'm Praising God*, *When God Sees Me Through*, *When I'm in His Presence*, *When I Hear His Call*, and *When God Calls Me Blessed*. This volume you now hold contains the "best of the best" of Anita Corrine Donihue's writings, carefully selected from all six of her beloved books.

A thread of thanksgiving weaves its way through all of Anita's writings. Whether she's basking in God's presence, listening closely for His leading, or sharing hymns of joy, Anita Corrine Donihue keeps her focus (and yours!) on the wonderful, loving heavenly Father who deserves all of our praise. We hope, by the time you finish this book, you'll be saying with Anita, *Thank You, Lord!*

THE EDITORS

Chapter 1

THANK YOU FOR LOVING ME

For you are the Fountain of life;
our light is from your Light.
Pour out your unfailing love
on those who know you!
Never stop giving your salvation
to those who long to do your will.

PSALM 36:9–10 TLB

"I am the true vine, and My Father is
the vinedresser."
"Abide in Me, and I in you."
"As the Father loved Me, I also have
loved you; abide in My love."

JOHN 15:1, 4, 9 NKJV

Heavenly Father, thank You for being so kind to me and for being my dearest friend. When I cry out and search for You, my God, You are here. When my parched soul thirsts for You during the droughts, You fill me to overflowing with living water. Thank You for making it possible to study Your Word and feed on it so I can be sustained and strengthened.

When I go to church and ask for Your presence, You bless me. When I rise at morn, labor throughout the day, and lie down at night, You are still with me. I praise You for satisfying my soul. How wonderful it is when I am able to turn to You anytime and sense Your holy presence. How great You are for aiding me through the challenges and trials that attack like noontime heat.

Without Your love and friendship, dear Lord, there would be a terrible void in my life nothing else could fill. Your loving-kindness is more wonderful than life itself.

I will bless You, my Lord. I will lift my heart and hands to You from whence comes my help. I will enter Your gates and give thanks to Your name. I will enter Your courts and praise You. You are the living God. You pump life into me each day. Praise be to You, O God!

Thank You, Lord Jesus, as You, the Lamb of God, feed me the water of life. Thank You for satisfying my soul. I praise You for filling me with blessings at Your table, for letting me scoop up living water from Your rivers of delight. Praise You for Your bountiful, measureless blessings.

WONDERFUL

Wonderful You are who made me.
Wonderful You are who knows me.
Wonderful You are who called me.
Wonderful You are who forgave me.
Wonderful You are who saved me.
Wonderful You are who leads me.
Wonderful is Your name.

God Treasures Me

Father, I praise You for treasuring me. Thank You for being my dearest friend and reminding me:

- When I felt worthless,
  You developed my abilities.

- When I felt I lacked beauty,
  You reminded me of the inner beauty
  You gave me.

- When I was unworthy,
  You showed me Your love and instilled
  worth in me.

- When I wept over my sins,
  You forgave me.

- When I tried and failed,
  You bridged the gap.

- When I felt I had nothing to offer,
  You saw potential in me.

- When others didn't seem to care,
  You adopted me as Your child,
  and You treasured me as Your own.

For Your Love, I Praise You

How I praise You, Lord God, for Your unlimited, overflowing, perfect love. How good You are! You are my Lord of lords. You are my God. There is no other. No one else is above You!

In return, I love You more than all else. For Your love, I praise Your holy name. Amen.

Awake, My Soul, to Joyful Lays

Awake, my soul, to joyful lays,
And sing thy great Redeemer's praise;
He justly claims a song from me—
His lovingkindness, O how free!
Lovingkindness, lovingkindness,
His lovingkindness, O how free!

When trouble, like a gloomy cloud,
Has gathered thick and thundered loud,
He near my soul has always stood—
His lovingkindness, O how good!
Lovingkindness, lovingkindness,
His lovingkindness, O how good!

SAMUEL MEDLEY, 1782

O Lord, thou hast searched me, and known me.
*   Thou knowest my downsitting and mine uprising,*
thou understandest my thought afar off.
*   Thou compassest my path and my lying down,*
and art acquainted with all my ways.
*   For there is not a word in my tongue,*
*   but, lo, O Lord, thou knowest it altogether.*
*   Thou hast beset me behind and before,*
*   and laid thine hand upon me.*
*   Such knowledge is too wonderful for me;*
*   it is high, I cannot attain unto it.*

PSALM 139:1–6 KJV

JESUS, THY BOUNDLESS LOVE TO ME

Jesus, Thy boundless love to me
    No thought can reach, no tongue declare;
Unite my thankful heart with Thee
    And reign without a rival there.
To Thee alone, dear Lord, I live;
    Myself to Thee, dear Lord, I give.

O love, how cheering is thy ray!
    All pain before thy presence flies;
Care, anguish, sorrow, melt away
    Wherever thy healing beams arise.
O Jesus, nothing may I see,
    Nothing desire or seek, but Thee!

PAUL GERHARDT, 1653
TRANSLATED BY JOHN WESLEY, 1739

ORANGE

It was early afternoon. Two of our sons and I had just arrived home from a regular day of school and work. Our youngest son, David, quickly completed his chores and homework and went out to have some fun with neighborhood friends. I started dinner simmering on the stove. Our elder son Jonathan was finishing up his homework at the dining room table.

Suddenly, David burst through the front door and ran to my side. "Mom, you really need to come help us out front."

David's tone of voice told me his request was important and couldn't wait. I quickly dried my hands, turned off the stove, and followed him out the door, with Jonathan on my heels.

I could see neighborhood kids clustered on our grass near the curb. When we reached the group, I was surprised to find the center of attention was the tiniest orange kitten I had ever seen away from its mother. It appeared to be injured. The children were trying desperately to help and had wrapped paper towels around the little creature. In spite of their efforts, the kitten shivered uncontrollably.

"What have we here?" I ventured.

David and his friends barely took their gaze from the kitty to tell me its horrible encounter. "Some big, black cat beat it up until we rescued it." One of the kids pointed to its miniature face covered with blood.

"Does it belong to anyone?" I asked.

The answer came back, a sad "No."

Sensing David and Jonathan holding their breath, my humanitarian instincts kicked in. "We'll take him in," I said. Jonathan gathered the little creature up, paper towels and all, and we took it inside.

In a matter of minutes, our family went into action. First, we said a prayer; then I grabbed a towel and handed it to Jonathan.

As I cooked dinner, my heart was warmed at the loving efforts put forth by our sons. Jonathan wrapped the shivering ball of fur in the towel and settled into our rocking chair. David knelt beside the chair, offering warm milk from his fingertip. The kitten kept shivering and didn't respond.

Jonathan snuggled it close to his chest, rocking and singing softly. Were we going to lose this little creature from shock? The boys refused to give up. Finally, after two hours of continuous TLC, the kitten stopped shivering and gingerly lapped the milk from David's finger.

Pleas to keep him were met with the words, "Only until we can find another home."

It took a lot of love from the whole family and plenty of care to nurse the little orange fluff ball back to health, but we succeeded. None of us was able, of course, to find it another home. The kitten gradually won the affection of everyone in our family, including my husband, Bob. Orange, the kitten would be called. That's how big it was. The size of a fluffy little orange.

Orange taught our family what compassion and tireless devotion are all about. The only way that kitten could have survived was by recognizing the help being given by two caring boys, and its being willing to accept and trust their love. Best of all was the pleasure Orange gave us as a part of our family.

<hr />

God has far more love for you and me than what we were capable of giving Orange. Isn't it wonderful how the Lord constantly cares about us as He offers His love and protection! The only way we can benefit, though, is to recognize and accept His love personally.

God is with us day and night, through good times and bad, no matter where we are. His love for us is measureless.

Love Comes from You

Lord, You often remind us to love and care for our families first. At times, we American families are so busy being thoughtful to those outside our homes that we forget the ones who are most important. Our families deserve our best manners, our best attention, and our first love, second to God.

Instead, at times, we forget our thoughtful and kind ways and mistreat each other. Perhaps we think our families will put up with our actions because they love us "just the way we are." Must we play mind games with or belittle and manipulate the ones we love? Must we say hurtful things to get our way or to get our points across? How sad. This must grieve You terribly, Lord. It is so wrong and so destructive. Forgive us for such sinful actions.

Help us treat our spouses, children, and other loved ones with kindness, to cherish and care for them. Help us to avoid careless words that may injure for a lifetime. May we treasure these dear ones and share their joys and concerns and dreams. May our foremost time and effort be with the ones we love the most. Let us show them the love we talk about so freely, so our families will grow strong and secure in You.

Lord, we know we cannot have strong family units without following Your teachings. You know our hearts. Let our lives please You.

LET YOUR LOVE REMAIN IN ME

Because of the love You shower upon me, Father, I love You. Thank You for being my dearest friend. How grateful I am that I can talk with You about anything in my life and know You never tire of listening. When I'm happy, You rejoice with me. When I'm discouraged or saddened, I feel You consoling me. When my body is racked with pain, I know You are here, strengthening and healing. When I carelessly say or do the wrong things, I experience Your correcting, yet loving and forgiving, presence.

Teach me, in turn, to love unconditionally, under any circumstances, as You love. If I were to possess every gift of Your Holy Spirit and not show love, I would only make phony, irritating noises. If I were able to prophesy or acquire all the wisdom of the ages and not show kindness, I wouldn't be worth a penny to You or others.

If I were blessed with an abundance of faith and could see people healed and all my prayers granted and not show compassion, it would all be for naught. If I were to give all my money and earthly goods to the needy and not show empathy, my offerings would be like filthy rags. If I were to be persecuted for speaking out for You and not respond with forgiveness, my words or actions would be of no substance.

Teach me love, patience, and kindness. When I feel slighted by others, Lord, I pray for graciousness to overcome any disappointment. Remind me to mix love with humility, rather than stealing the attention of others and bragging. Encourage me not to be egotistical, critical, selfish, jealous, or rude. Help me not to put other people down but to lift them up.

When someone hurts my feelings, please strongly remind me to not hold a grudge. Instead, teach me, Lord, to overlook others' faults and lift them to You in prayer for help and encouragement. Teach me to pray for the salvation of those who spitefully use me. I don't need to worry about revenge. Instead, I place it all in Your hands.

Grant me the strength to be a loyal friend even when others are in the depths of sin or despair. Show me how to look beyond their problems and see their needs. Let me assure them that when they're hurting I still believe in them and look for the best they can do. Help me to be considerate, aware that my deeds are in the best interest of my friends.

The spiritual gifts and talents You give are precious, and I thank You for them. Most of all, though, I ask for Your love, that I may pass it on to others.

I don't understand all the mysteries of life, nor do I possess tremendous intelligence or ability. I don't have answers to the world's great problems. But I can exercise Your wonderful, powerful love. When life's challenges come, I will remember that love through You conquers all. In the midst of everything we go through here on earth with its joys and sorrows, I long to see You face-to-face in all Your glorious completeness. It is then I will be able to ask You infinite questions and experience Your victorious love and joy in heaven.

Thank You for the faith, the hope, and the tenderness You give me, Lord. Thank You most of all for Your abiding love. Let Your love remain in me and my love remain in You forever.

Love Divine, All Loves Excelling

Jesus, Thou art all compassion,
Pure unbounded love Thou art;
Visit us with Thy salvation;
Enter every trembling heart.

CHARLES WESLEY, 1747

O God, thou art my God;
  early will I seek thee: my soul thirsteth for
  thee, my flesh longeth for thee in a dry and
  thirsty land, where no water is;
To see thy power and thy glory,
  so as I have seen thee in the sanctuary.
Because thy lovingkindness is better than life,
  my lips shall praise thee.
Thus will I bless thee while I live:
  I will lift up my hands in thy name.
My soul shall be satisfied as with marrow
  and fatness; and my mouth shall praise thee
  with joyful lips:
When I remember thee upon my bed,
  and meditate on thee in the night watches.
Because thou hast been my help,
  therefore in the shadow of thy wings
  will I rejoice.

PSALM 63:1–7 KJV

Be imitators of God, therefore, as dearly
loved children and live a life of love, just as
Christ loved us and gave himself up for us
as a fragrant offering and sacrifice to God.

EPHESIANS 5:1–2 NIV

Chapter 2

THANK YOU FOR SAVING ME

"I am the way and the truth and the life. No one comes to the Father except through me."

JOHN 14:6 NIV

But when the kindness and love of God our Savior appeared, he saved us, not because of righteous things we had done, but because of his mercy.

TITUS 3:4–5 NIV

SAVIOR, PRINCE OF PEACE

Thank You, Lord Jesus, for being my Savior, my Prince of Peace. I praise You for breaking the power of sin and death and leading me into everlasting life. Through this, You have given me peace of heart and mind and a wonderful heritage in the family of God, our Father.

I can't comprehend how Your life-giving Spirit has made it possible for me to live forever. It is so wonderful. I need not fear the future, for my life is in Your hands. Thank You for the peace You give when life's uncertainties arise. I need not fear physical death, for I will be taken to be with You in glory. How awesome! How magnificent!

You are truly holy, Lord Jesus. You have been and are forever. You are my mighty God, my King above all rulers, my eternal Lord. I worship and praise Your name forever.

BEHOLD, WHAT LOVE!

Behold, what love, what boundless love,
The Father hath bestowed
On sinners lost, that we should be
Now called "the sons of God!"

ROBERT BOSWELL, 1746-1804

REDEEMER

Praise You, O Lord, for being my Savior, my Redeemer. Thank You for snatching me from a life of sin and hiding me safely in Your everlasting arms.

Because You live forever and You saw fit to love me, You have redeemed me and given me a wonderful life as Your child. I live because You live. I am free from sin because You set me free. Thank You for giving me joy indescribable and power to win a victorious life above the trials of this world. This gladness You give me each day would be out of my reach without my knowing You as my Redeemer.

Thank You for preparing a greater place for me and an unquenchable everlasting joy. The way to heaven would be impossible for me to find without You.

I lift my heart in praise to You, my Lord: my Way, my Truth, my Life, my Redeemer.

> *Let the words of my mouth, and the*
> *meditation of my heart, be acceptable in*
> *thy sight, O LORD, my strength, and my*
> *redeemer.*

> PSALM 19:14 KJV

How can we grasp the tremendous love Jesus had for us when He obeyed His Father's call to come to earth? Heaven, in all its splendor and glory, was His home. There He knew no sin, no tears, and no suffering. Then He was called to this earth, a place in stark contrast to His heavenly home.

Certainly, Jesus knew the perfect, eternal plan and what His Father had sent Him to do. No doubt, the Savior fully realized the suffering, pain, and the humility of bearing our sins that He would have to endure on our behalf. Jesus, the Son of God, was there with His Father even before Adam and Eve were created.

According to God's plan, Jesus obediently came in the form of a helpless infant to a loving, God-fearing, earthly mother and stepfather. From the day of His birth, those who wished to destroy Jesus searched relentlessly for the child.

While growing up, Jesus perceived things in life far beyond His years. He must have often felt isolated and lonely because He was different from everyone else. There were certainly times when Mary and Joseph were perplexed at Jesus' actions. The significance of the Son of God in their care went far beyond their imagination.

During His ministry, Jesus loved with an unlimited, perfect love. He felt the hurts of others, sometimes weeping Himself. He abhorred evil with a sanctified hatred. He constantly reached out and helped others, often to the point of exhaustion. And He prayed intensely for those who would follow Him.

Neither pray I for these alone, but for them also which shall believe on me through their word. I in them, and thou in me, that they may be made perfect in one; and that the world may know that thou hast sent me, and hast loved them, as thou hast loved me. And I have declared unto them thy name, and will declare it: that the love wherewith thou hast loved me may be in them, and I in them.

JOHN 17:20, 23, 26 KJV

Jesus left Jerusalem and crossed over the Kidron Brook to the Garden of Gethsemane in order to pray. His disciples went with Him. Although He begged them to support Him in prayer, they soon disappointed Him by falling asleep.

The Son of God petitioned His Father about many things during that time in the garden. He was so intense and filled with care that perspiration and tears flowed down His face. Even though the Savior dreaded the upcoming suffering and shame, He had enough love to plead for all of us.

When I Survey the Wondrous Cross

See from His head, His hands, His feet,
Sorrow and love flow mingled down!
Did e'er such love and sorrow meet,
Or thorns compose so rich a crown?

ISAAC WATTS, 1707

*This is love for God: to obey his commands.
And his commands are not burdensome,
for everyone born of God overcomes the
world. This is the victory that has overcome
the world, even our faith. Who is it that
overcomes the world? Only he who believes
that Jesus is the Son of God.*

1 JOHN 5:3–5 NIV

CHRIST'S FORGIVENESS

In the midst of the darkness and gloom of the cross, there came a voice from one of those thieves. It flashed into the soul of Jesus as He hung there, "This must be more than man; this must be the true Messiah." He cried out, "Lord, remember me when Thou comest into Thy Kingdom!"

We are anxious to get the last word of our dying friends. Here was the last act of Jesus. He snatched the thief from the jaws of death by saying, "Today you will be with Me in Paradise" (Luke 23:43 NKJV).

Such was His forgiveness of sin an act of grace, just as His forgiveness of His murderers was an act of mercy.

DWIGHT L. MOODY

Where Is the Key?

Where is the key to a close relationship with Jesus Christ? Is it begging His royal presence? Reading the Bible for hours throughout the day? In sacrifice and service? Do any of these things earn merit in God's sight? Do lengthy prayers?

Christ Himself is the key. We must allow Him to turn the lock to every room in our hearts, then fling wide the door and let Him enter. He already knows about the hidden dirt and dust bunnies in the corners. He is well aware of thoughts and actions that displease Him. We must allow Jesus not only to enter but also to bring His broom, mop, and plenty of soap!

Jesus has a way of cleansing and renewing. He can change sinful, rotten ways to a clean, sweet-smelling fragrance unto Him.

Jesus is not a mere image or a lovely picture on our wall. He is our living Savior. He wants to be our dearest friend. When the Lord Jesus is totally welcome to every room in our lives, we will truly know His presence and be able to walk closely with Him.

I will bless the LORD at all times:
  his praise shall continually be in my mouth.
My soul shall make her boast in the LORD:
  the humble shall hear thereof, and be glad.
O magnify the LORD with me,
  and let us exalt his name together.
I sought the LORD, and he heard me,
  and delivered me from all my fears.

This poor man cried, and the LORD heard him,
  and saved him out of all his troubles.
The angel of the LORD encampeth round about
  them that fear him, and delivereth them.
O taste and see that the LORD is good:
  blessed is the man that trusteth in him.

The young lions do lack, and suffer hunger:
  but they that seek the LORD
  shall not want any good thing.
The eyes of the LORD are upon the righteous,
  and his ears are open unto their cry.

The righteous cry, and the LORD heareth,
  and delivereth them out of all their troubles.
The LORD is nigh unto them that are of
  a broken heart; and saveth such as be
  of a contrite spirit.

PSALM 34:1–4, 6–8, 10, 15, 17–18 KJV

King of Kings

There are crowns worn by living monarchs, of which it would be difficult to estimate the value. The price paid for their jewels is the least part of it. They cost thousands of lives and rivers of human blood; yet in His esteem, and surely in ours also, Christ's crown outweighs them all. He gave His life for it; and alone, of all monarchs, He was crowned at His coronation by the hands of Death. Others cease to be kings when they die. By dying, He became a king. He entered His kingdom through the gates of the grave and ascended the universe by the steps of a cross.

Thomas Guthrie

LORD, ENTHRONED IN HEAVENLY SPLENDOR

Lord, enthroned in heavenly splendor,
    First begotten from the dead.
Thou alone, our strong defender,
    Liftest up Thy people's head.

Here our humblest homage pay we,
    Here in loving reverence bow;
Here for faith's discernment pray we,
    Lest we fail to know Thee now.

Alleluia! Alleluia! Alleluia!

GEORGE HUGH BOURNE, 1874

But he was pierced for our transgressions,
    he was crushed for our iniquities;
the punishment that brought us peace
    was upon him,
    and by his wounds we are healed.

ISAIAH 53:5 NIV

GIVE OF YOUR BEST TO THE MASTER

Give of your best to the Master;
Naught else is worthy His love.
He gave Himself for your ransom,
Gave up His glory above.

Laid down His life without murmur,
You from sin's ruin to save.
Give Him your heart's adoration;
Give Him the best that you have.

HOWARD B. GROSE, 1851–1939

*For God so loved the world, that he gave
his only begotten Son, that whosoever
believeth in him should not perish,
but have everlasting life. For God sent
not his Son into the world to condemn
the world; but that the world through
him might be saved.*

JOHN 3:16–17 KJV

Chapter 3

THANK YOU FOR BLESSING ME

Oh. . .give thanks to the LORD for His
goodness,
And for His wonderful works to the
children of men!
For He satisfies the longing soul,
And fills the hungry soul with goodness.

PSALM 107:8–9 NKJV

HE GIVETH MORE GRACE

His love has no limit, His grace has no measure,
His power no boundary known unto men;
For out of His infinite riches in Jesus,
He giveth, and giveth, and giveth again!

ANNIE JOHNSON FLINT, 1866–1932

LOOK FOR THE LITTLE THINGS

Are you searching for God's blessings,
    Trying hard to find just one?
Are you walking in the shadows,
    Hanging on till day is done?

Do you fail to see the wonder
    That God offers you each day?
Do you notice all He bestows?
    All the joy He sends your way?

God gives many kinds of blessings,
    Through the little things we see.
He turns shadows into sunlight,
    Hued with rainbow, rose, and tree.

God breaks dullness with bright laughter,
    Or a child's sweet, simple deed.
He grants wonders unexpectedly.
    His surprises meet each need.

When you notice the little things—
    His blessings, all around,
When you're glad for what each day brings,
    Then your happiness abounds.

Feel caresses from spring breezes,
    Smell the freshness in His rain.
Step out at night and watch the stars
    Shoot across the sky again.

Arise before the sun comes up,
    View a glorious orange display,
Revealing waking signs of life,
    That welcome a brand-new day.

Keep looking for the little things.
    God's blessings will come to you,
Filling your heart with peace and joy,
    And making your life brand-new.

Thank You for the Little Blessings

Father, sometimes I go along full speed ahead, not looking right or left. I may forget to look up to You and be aware of Your small blessings. Numerous things I must accomplish (or seemingly so) crowd out the most important gifts You have planned.

Please remind me, Lord, to keep watching for Your everyday miniblessings. When I'm buried under responsibilities and feel life just isn't all that great, I want to be mindful of the little things keeping the joy in my life.

Perhaps simple, split-second blessings in a busy day are more than insignificant. They often turn out to be the most treasured times of my life.

Thank You, Lord.

God Moves in a Mysterious Way

God moves in a mysterious way
His wonders to perform;
He plants His footsteps in the sea
And rides upon the storm.

Ye fearful saints, fresh courage take;
The clouds ye so much dread
Are big with mercy and shall break
In blessings on your head.

WILLIAM COWPER, 1774

"Consider the lilies of the field, how they grow: they neither toil nor spin; and yet I say to you that even Solomon in all his glory was not arrayed like one of these.

"But seek first the kingdom of God and His righteousness, and all these things shall be added to you. Therefore do not worry about tomorrow, for tomorrow will worry about its own things. Sufficient for the day is its own trouble."

MATTHEW 6:28–29, 33–34 NKJV

Beautiful Music

Thank You, Lord, for the beautiful music in
    my life.
The whistling teakettle in the early
    morning chill.
The soft whooshing of the furnace
    blowing warm air through the house.
The chirp of an energetic robin outside our
    window.
The purring of our kitty awaiting his breakfast.
The singing of my husband in the shower.
The Christian music on the radio when I'm on
    my way to work.
The still, ever presence of Your voice
    throughout the day.
The tender greeting from my husband after
    work.
The kids wrestling and playing in the evening.
The soft tone of my sons before bed: "Good
    night, Mom. I love you."
I hear my echo. "I love you, too."

Some of our experiences in life are dangerous physically, others spiritually. No doubt many of us have been blessed by God's rescuing hand more than once. Although we may have earned a few of His blessings, all of them are given by His gracious love.

How thankful we can be for those who risk their lives for others, especially for strangers. We can be grateful for the faithful, everyday loving prayer warriors who quietly care and love and give of themselves.

The graciousness and love God bestows on us is far greater than the good things we do. In spite of our good-hearted efforts, the only way we can gain His favor or our way to heaven is by accepting Him and actively acknowledging Him as our personal Savior and Lord.

He is the Creator of all. He is the One who placed within us the love and compassion we share with each other.

We don't understand or have control of our futures. But one thing we can know for sure is that God loves and cares for us. No matter what turn our lives take, we can seek Him. As we open our hearts, He can help us. The more we submit to His will, the more He is able to work through us. Each time He does, God blesses our lives beyond measure.

Count Your Blessings

When upon life's billows you are tempest tossed,
When you are discouraged, thinking all is lost,
Count your many blessings, name them one by one,
And it will surprise you what the Lord hath done.

Are you ever burdened with a load of care?
Does the cross seem heavy you are called to bear?
Count your many blessings, every doubt will fly,
And you will keep singing as the days go by.

So, amid the conflict whether great or small,
Do not be disheartened, God is over all;
Count your many blessings, angels will attend,
Help and comfort give you to your journey's end.

Count your blessings, name them one by one,
Count your blessings, see what God hath done!
Count your blessings, name them one by one,
And it will surprise you what the Lord hath done.

Johnson Oatman Jr., 1897

A Willing Spirit

She suffers from poor health but never gives up. Sometimes walking becomes too painful, and she's forced to use a wheelchair or walker. When she's able to come to church, though, she's there. She's always willing to listen to the concerns of others, to care and pray for them. She doesn't sing in a choir, teach a class, or give dynamic speeches. She's just approachable, loving, compassionate.

Even when she's home, she's helping others. She sends notes to the sick, the bereaved, and the lonely. She sews banners for the Sunday school department. She helps with paperwork. She shows a huge amount of love and cooks great dishes for church potlucks.

Thank you, Sharon, for being a willing spirit for the Lord!

How fortunate we all are to have the loving, willing spirits who bless us each day.

Make Me Forever Willing

When You call me, Father, make me eager to do Your will. Help me to be dependable and finish the work You set before me. Let me jump in with eager enthusiasm to complete the task, as though I'm doing it for You.

If my spirit grows weary and my body becomes tired, grant me the strength I need. Help me to be willing to listen, love, and care.

I'm ready to do anything for You, Father. Please stay close so we can be a blessing together.

The Giver of All

Thank You, Father, for being the Giver of all. My possessions, the people I love, the beauties of nature—You are the One who gave them. There would be nothing without You. You made life. You are the Beginning. You are the greatest Giver.

I praise You for the beauty You furnish us on this earth. The skies, trees, and flowers come from You. The sun, moon, and stars reflect Your handiwork.

Thank You for making me the way I am. You had a plan when You created me. I'm grateful for my family, loved ones, and friends. Thank You for teaching us to love one another. Thank You for Your church, for the strength and encouragement it gives.

I praise You especially for Your pure, everlasting love demonstrated by the giving of Your Son, so I may be a part of the family of God.

Teach me, O Lord, to give with a love like Yours. Guide me, I pray, into ways I can give to others with my actions, talents, time, and riches. Let me do these things and give You all the glory.

In Jesus' name, amen.

God's Blessings Be upon You

May you lift your gaze to the heavens
    and hunger for the Lord, your God.
May your help come from Him,
    the Maker of all creation.

May He not let your feet slip
    outside of His holy ways.
May He keep you safe day and night,
    for He never rests.

May He encompass you
    as you go out and come in.
May the Lord be your shade by day
    so the sun will not harm you.

May He be your shelter
    when the moon shimmers by night.
May He protect you with His mighty hand
    and watch over you—now and forevermore.
Amen.

God Bless You!

"God bless you!" from the heart we sing,
God gives to ev'ryone His grace;
Till He on high His ransomed bring
To dwell with Him in endless peace.

God bless you on your pilgrim way,
Thro' storm and sunshine guiding still;
His presence guard you day by day,
And keep you safe from ev'ry ill.

God bless you in this world of strife,
When oft the soul would homeward fly,
And give the sweetness to your life,
Of waiting for the rest on high.

God bless you! And the patience give
To walk thro' life by Jesus' side;
For Him to bear, for Him to live,
And then with Him be glorified.

El Nathan, 1840–1901

Thank You for the different kinds of blessings You give me, Father. Not just material riches people often think of but also Your blessings that last forever.

Thank You for Your blessing of guidance. Each year, I trust Your advice more. You fill my thoughts with Your heavenly purpose.

I don't have time to worry about whether I will be rich or famous in the eyes of man, because You have given me a work to do for You. I realize life is short, Lord. I can't waste it. Help me budget my time like a carefully balanced bankbook. When I accomplish a little more for Your kingdom, I feel wealthier than a millionaire.

Thank You for blessing me with a heart filled with joy. How rich I feel to hear Your call to serve. Because of this, I place my spiritual treasures in heaven. Nothing can snatch them away, nor do they rust or wear out. Your spiritual treasures will even last beyond this fragile physical life of mine and go on forever!

I don't know if You will grant me worldly riches. If You do, I will praise You and try to be a good steward. My focus is on You, my Lord, not on love of money. I enjoy the material blessings You grant me, but I don't want to become corrupt and make them my idol.

Your blessings are more wonderful than the finest gems! Thank You for them. Please help me remember throughout my life to invest in heavenly things and keep my heart fixed there.

Through all this, I praise You for material blessings, comfort, ease, and joy indescribable. How amazing it is when I pass some of these blessings on to others. You return them to me, pressed down and overflowing with Your love.

> *I love those who love me,*
> *   and those who seek me find me.*
> *With me are riches and honor,*
> *   enduring wealth and prosperity.*
> *My fruit is better than fine gold;*
> *   what I yield surpasses choice silver.*
> *I walk in the way of righteousness,*
> *   along the paths of justice,*
> *bestowing wealth on those who love me*
> *   and making their treasuries full.*

PROVERBS 8:17–21 NIV

Thank You for Your Goodness

Thank You for Your goodness and blessings, Lord. Your mercy and kindness surpass all. During these trying times, I turn to You. I am amazed how You used different people in my life to intervene and help me safely through. I praise You, Lord, for working so many things out and caring for me. Thank You for being with me from the very day I was born and for how You are with me all my life.

The Lord's My Shepherd, I'll Not Want

My table Thou hast furnished
In presence of my foes;
My head Thou dost with oil anoint,
And my cup overflows.

F. Rous, *Scottish Psalter*, 1650

Chapter 4

THANK YOU FOR BEING FAITHFUL

It is good to praise the Lord
and make music to your name,
O Most High,
to proclaim your love in the morning
and your faithfulness at night.

PSALM 92:1–2 NIV

For I am convinced that nothing can ever
separate us from his love. Death can't, and life
can't. The angels won't, and all the powers of
hell itself cannot keep God's love away.

Our fears for today, our worries about to-
morrow, or where we are—high above the sky,
or in the deepest ocean—nothing will ever be able
to separate us from the love of God demonstrated
by our Lord Jesus Christ when he died for us.

ROMANS 8:38–39 TLB

GREAT IS THY FAITHFULNESS

Great is Thy faithfulness!
Great is Thy faithfulness!
Morning by morning new mercies I see.
All I have needed Thy hand hath provided;
Great is Thy faithfulness, Lord, unto me!

THOMAS OBEDIAH CHISHOLM, 1923

I Will Remember Your Faithfulness

Through my life's changing sands of time, I look back and recall Your countless blessings, Father. Thank You for being with me through all my years.

I praise You for Your faithfulness in helping me to adjust to life's changes and for granting me strength to trust in You. Your love has always been there for me. Even when I felt abandoned and believed things were hopeless, You helped me through. Afterward, I looked back and often saw how You had worked.

Thank You for Your unchanging love. It goes above the mountains and beyond the skies to help me. It reaches into the deepest sea, where You stretch out Your hand and lift me up.

Because I see what You have done for me in the past, I look to the future without fear. Thank You, Lord God. In all my days, I will always remember Your faithfulness.

Loud and Clear

I thought February 28, 2001, would be like any other day teaching first and second graders. That is, except for one thing. I was expecting an important phone call from Paul, a publishing company editorial director, and twelve sales representatives. They would be interviewing me about my books. The call was scheduled to come into the faculty room phone booth during my lunch break, at 11:20 a.m. (PST), to be precise. Wendy, the teacher I assist, and I had worked out the details ahead of time so I could easily slip down the hall.

Language arts lessons with my small group around the table ran in a smooth sequence. Every once in a while, however, I found myself glancing at the clock. Now it was 10:50, only a half hour to go.

An abrupt sound like something hitting the side of the school building jolted us from our work.

"Earthquake!" I tried to sound calm, but the words came out as a shout.

"Everyone, under the tables," Wendy ordered.

The students responded immediately. We had gone through the drill many times and were pleased to see the children do exactly as they had been taught.

—⊷⊷⊷—

For fifteen to thirty seconds, everything violently heaved and rolled, not letting up. Wendy and I knew the longer the quake, the more serious the outcome.

Quiet whimpers and anxious whispers came from the children.

I tried to hold them close with one arm, like a hen gathering her chicks, and hold on to the table leg with my other hand. I didn't want to lose hold of the worktable, as it was our primary shelter from possible falling debris.

Of course, it didn't take long for me to pray about our frightening situation. "God, keep these children safe and watch over my family," I urgently whispered.

My students nestling near me didn't seem to be aware of my almost-silent prayer. They already knew by our everyday examples that both Wendy and I loved the Lord.

After almost a minute, the shaking began to slow down. The room, though, felt like a huge, sloshy water bed. One little boy in my group acted more frightened than the others. His little body shook as he leaned against me.

"Shane, do you want me to hug you?"

"Yes," he squeaked.

I let go of the table leg and wrapped both arms around him and the others in my group as the tremors finally began to subside. "It's going to be all right," I assured them.

We were to remain under the table until the all-clear announcement blared from the classroom speaker, a length of time that seemed endless. Finally, the message came through, and we crawled out from under the furniture. After the initial shock, everyone went into action, checking on the safety of our children and the structure of the building. Thank God, no injuries were reported and there appeared to be no significant damage to the building.

I glanced once again at the clock. It was 11:15. I attempted to phone a family member, with no success. Then I tried calling the publishing company's 800 number to warn them about the phone lines. Still no success. I knew it would be a miracle if Paul's phone call made it through.

I hurried to the school office where the phones were ringing off the hooks. When I asked Tami if she had received the call, I couldn't believe what I was saying. *What a silly question,* I thought. How could it be possible?

Tami had one receiver held to her ear and frantically pointed to another phone. "Line one," she announced.

"I can't believe it!" I exclaimed. I hurried to the faculty room and found the surprisingly vacant phone booth. I shut the door and picked up the receiver.

"This is Anita. Paul, is that you? Yes, I can hear you." I sighed with relief. "You're coming in loud and clear. We just had an earthquake here. Yes, we're all right but a bit shaken up."

The interview went well. The Spirit of the Lord Jesus Christ vibrated through the lines during the next fifteen minutes as we talked.

I thought of the editor and sales team that evening as the national news covered extensive damage in our area and for miles around. I felt sure the company's team was also watching and keeping us in their prayers. For that, I felt grateful.

God taught me a lesson that day. No matter what kind of chaos, danger, or uncertainty is going on, our Lord is still right by our side. I believe He's wrapping His arms around us and assuring us of His love and care.

More miraculous than the editor's phone call is the way God cuts through obstructions in our world. No matter what, He still makes it possible for us to hear His call. Loud and clear.

My Hope Is in Your Faithfulness

Lord, I thank You for Your unfailing faithfulness. Because of Your kindness, I know I shall never be consumed. Because of Your compassion, I know I shall never be alone. Because of Your mercy, I shall always have hope.

Every day as I quietly wait for Your direction, You shed new mercies on me. Every night, You give me portions of Your everlasting peace and joy.

Thank You, Lord, for always being with me. You are the solid rock on which I stand!

END OF THE ROPE

Are you at the end of your rope,
Struggling with strife and pain?
Do you feel you can't hang on
For whatever you might gain?

Do your sufferings overshadow
Everything that is good?
You'll find that at the end of the rope
God provides all that's good.

Are you at the end of your rope
With a load you cannot bear?
No matter how hard you struggle or try,
Does nobody seem to care?

Do you beg for strength to hold on,
When your being aches with pain?
You'll find that at the end of the rope
God is waiting, once again.

There at the end of your rope,
You'll see God's work is best.
There you can learn His answers for life,
While letting Him work out the rest.

If your goals and dreams are changing,
Your heart and mind renewed,
You've found that at the end of the rope
God lovingly cares for you.

How can our minds grasp all the issues we are concerned about? From earthquakes, floods, and tornadoes to poverty, war, illness, and death, the list goes on and on.

We worry and speculate, but it seems to do us little good. Although we need to be responsible for our families and world problems, we must recognize *we* are not in control. *God is.*

Things may not always turn out the way we want. Our prayers may even appear to go unanswered. When we wonder why circumstances happen the way they do, we must remember that God truly loves us and cares about our every need, whether small or large.

Later, we can look back and see the hand of God moving in ways we never dreamed. We are often amazed at how He saw the bigger picture, when we were only able to perceive one tiny dot.

When fear, uncertainty, and anxiety flood over you, ask God to wipe away the worry and replace it with openhearted worship to Him. He has a magnificent way of faithfully fitting everything together for good and bountifully blessing us when we place our trust in Him.

This can be a difficult step to take when life is really tough. Just as when we took our first steps holding a parent's hand, so it is when we appear pretty wobbly that God is always with us, ready to hold our hands and give us balance. We don't have to attempt these steps all at once. One tiny step of faith. One tiny phrase spoken in worship to Him.

When life crashes down on me, as it sometimes does, I look back on the many blessings God has given me. I think especially of the most fearful, uncertain experiences and how He brought me through them in such miraculous ways. Then I try to mentally take the problems and place them in my clenched fist. I shakily open my palm, lay my concerns before the Lord, and ask Him to do whatever He wants with them. I pray for faith—I don't try to dictate my will for the outcome or timing. Then I say seven little words:

"Your will be done, Lord, not mine."

Once is not enough. Often I need to pray these words for my own sake again and again. As time goes on, I experience His assuring presence. I begin to recognize His loving faithfulness at work in my life.

We may feel unworthy to receive God's awesome blessings. Do we even deserve them? The answer is that Jesus paid the price for our sins. *He* is the One who makes the blessings possible.

- Trust completely in God.
- Accept His bountiful blessings.
- Be thankful.

We Do

The church was packed with friends as the simple ceremony began. Bob and I stepped forward and faced Pastor Jerry Phillips. My father stood by my other side, and we were flanked by four young men. Our friend Phil sang a lovely song; then Bob and I sang to each other.

Bob and I gazed into each other's love-struck eyes as Pastor Jerry led us through our vows. I was thrilled to my toes. Two of the young men presented us with our rings. Bob and I exchanged our tokens of love.

Pastor Jerry reminded us of the sanctity of marriage. His words went deep into our hearts. Then came the part, "Who gives this woman to be married to this man?"

A deep, reverent, "We do," chorused from my father and our four grown sons. We paused and prayed, thanking God for the lifetime of marriage and family He has given us. Bob and I hugged and kissed at the end of renewing our vows in celebration of our fortieth wedding anniversary.

Forty years, and we love each other more than ever. He still looks at me with a sparkle in his eyes. He opens doors for me, rubs my back, and buys me flowers. My heart still goes pitter-patter when he enters a room. When we go somewhere together, I still dress to look my best for my sweetheart and friend.

Our anniversary was more than a celebration of forty years of marriage. It was a celebration of life in Jesus Christ with the ones we love the most: each other, our sons, our daughters-in-love, our grandchildren, our parents, our family of God. Most of all, we celebrated our love for the Lord, the Author and Finisher of it all.

I'll Sing Your Praises

I'll sing Your praises all my days,
Though my rhythm may be slow,
In weary tune, I lift my song,
Your Spirit I now know.

Lord, when life's shadows cross my sky,
And the sun is not in view,
I still sing out in faltering voice,
My praises unto You.

May I keep singing all my days,
Though my voice is stretched and thin,
The bubbling, joyous waters stir
From Your Spirit deep within.

Let others hear my singing, Lord.
Let Your glory ring out clear.
And may they say, "I, too, shall sing,
Throughout my span of years."

Chapter 5

THANK YOU FOR FORGIVENESS

"Come now, and let us reason together,"
says the LORD,
"Though your sins are like scarlet,
They shall be as white as snow;
Though they are red like crimson,
They shall be as wool.
If you are willing and obedient,
you shall eat the good of the land."

ISAIAH 1:18–19 NKJV

"But when you are praying, first forgive
anyone you are holding a grudge against,
so that your Father in heaven will forgive
you your sins too."

MARK 11:25 TLB

CREATE IN ME A STAINLESS HEART

O Lord, my God, have mercy upon me, I pray. Though I try to do what is right, I often fall short. I can't build a victorious life without You. Forgive me of my shortcomings and wrong attitudes. I long to be acceptable in Your sight.

Sprinkle Your cleansing blood upon my heart. Wash and make me as white as snow. Refine me. Skim off my faults and make Your child pure like glistening gold. Create in me a stainless heart, O Lord. Restore a just spirit within my soul. Thank You for not losing patience or giving up on one such as I. Fill me with Your Holy Spirit and restore to my life the joy of Your salvation.

As You and I begin this new quest in life, I pray for You to help me be careful and obedient in all I think, say, and do. I want to exalt You with my whole being, Lord.

I will sing with joy about Your love and forgiveness. My lips will constantly praise You through every adventure of my life. I want to pass on Your good news to all who are willing to listen.

Thank You, Lord, for being my Savior!

Helping Me Forgive

Lord, thank You for helping me praise You in my most broken and angry moments. How can I forgive, Lord, when I am cut down and mistreated repeatedly? I know You say seventy times seven, but I don't have it in my heart to do so. I again call upon You for help. Although I don't want to forgive, Lord, I ask You to change my heart.

Little by little, I feel You peel away the layers of bitterness. Like a big, smelly onion, my angry spirit is a sting and irritant to the souls around me and even to myself. This must hurt You, too, Lord, to see me like this. I'm beginning to realize my unforgiveness separates me from You.

How can I get over the pain and frustration? It has grown and festered into a huge spiritual and emotional boil. It eats away at me to the point that I feel physically ill. I don't want to be like this, Lord. Although the process of Your working in me is as painful as lancing an infected boil, I pray for You to cleanse, forgive, and heal me.

Thank You for helping me to back off so I can look at all these hurts with a better perspective. Evil has been manipulating not only my offenders, but me, too. Thank You for giving me the insight to pray for those who spitefully use me. Please help them to accept You as their Savior. I pray for them to be set free from wrongdoing so they, too, may experience Your joy-filled, abundant life.

Thank You for showing me how to love them with a love that comes from You, even when all is not right. I realize now I don't have to agree with them in order to forgive. I don't have to set myself up for them to continue to hurt me, nor do I need to unwisely trust them. But I must forgive, even if they aren't sorry or haven't changed.

Thank You for teaching me to let go and turn it all over to You. Your wisdom will work in their lives.

Thank You for helping me see where I have erred. You are teaching me to admit where I'm wrong and, if needed, to ask forgiveness. What if my apology is not accepted? Then I leave it in Your hands, Lord.

You have showed me the answer is not whether all is resolved. The answer is for You to create a pure, clean heart in me. I must do right in Your eyes and leave the rest in Your hands. I must forgive as You have forgiven me. After all this, I trust and praise You for Your wisdom and love.

If hurts return, I again take them to You and lay them at Your feet. You are my Healer, Redeemer, Counselor, Defender, and my Source of peace and strength. Thank You, Lord. Praise be to You!

Forbearing one another, and forgiving one another. . .even as Christ forgave you, so also do ye.

COLOSSIANS 3:13 KJV

Thank You for Taking Me Back

Father, I was just like that younger son who packed his bags, took his inheritance, and left his father, choosing a life of sin in a faraway land. After loving and serving You, I also chose to go astray and dabble in the sins of this world.

Thank You for freely taking me back with open arms when I came running to You with a repentant heart. Thank You for all You have done for me and for Your wonderful, forgiving love. Your mercy is so rich. You gave me life again. How I praise You!

Thank You for forgiving me—again. I cannot comprehend how You never hold a grudge against me. Instead, I know my sins are completely washed away. Your love is far greater than how high the heavens are above this little round ball called Earth. Your love stretches farther than the east is from the west. Thank You for being my tender, understanding Father.

I praise You over and over, Lord. Once I was lost. Now I am found and rejoice as a part of the family of God. I can finally see what real love is in You, Christ Jesus, my Savior. Thank You for welcoming me home.

Barney and Paul were good friends. Their close friendship made them like brothers. They went to church, prayed, and felt God call them to serve on the mission field together.

The two men's personalities were completely opposite, however. Barney had a loving, caring way, always trying to encourage people to seek God. Paul told people about Jesus with vigor and drive. He had total focus on the most efficient way he could spread the gospel to as many people as possible. Both men served God to the best of their abilities.

On one of their mission trips, Barney decided to bring his cousin Mark along. Partway through the trip, Mark told the two friends he wanted to go back home. Barney and Paul continued their work of winning souls for the Lord.

A new mission trip was planned. Barney wanted to continue encouraging Mark by bringing him along again. Paul reminded Barney how Mark had abandoned them before, and he gave a firm, "No." Tempers rose. Harsh words were spoken. Barney and Paul decided to go their separate ways.

As you can probably tell by now, this modern-day story spins off from the Bible, telling about Paul, Barnabas, and Mark (Acts 15:36–41). Hurt feelings must have been deep.

None of us really know what God's will was for Paul or Barnabas. God certainly must have hurt for them. In spite of it all, God blessed each of their ministries. In time, their wounds healed.

Sometimes Christians disagree, many feeling they are led of God. After struggling to work things out, they give up and go their separate ways. They may try to make things right, but the hurts go too deep.

When this happens, our concerns must be brought to God and left for Him to handle. God can help us forgive, even if the other person isn't sorry. Not forgiving is destructive. When we allow Him, God creates a new work within us, making a pure heart, free from bitterness and acceptable to Him. This can be done only when we call upon God for His power and love. We wait on God while He deals with our lives and the lives of those who hurt us. We realize we must change where we're wrong. We must forgive, let the faults of others go, and pray for these people. It may take time to heal. However, God has an amazing way of turning our bungles and poor attitudes around. He can do remarkable things in our lives.

In spite of everything, God has the love and compassion to bless those who long to serve Him. He works things out simultaneously for good in what is best for us and for others, when we obey Him. Paul later wrote, in Colossians 4:10 NIV: "My fellow prisoner Aristarchus sends you his greetings, as does Mark, the cousin of Barnabas. (You have received instructions about him; if he comes to you, welcome him.)"

Father, before I gave my heart to You, my life had no direction or meaning. I was going nowhere fast. Then You spoke to me. You kept urging me to give my all to You. I could not. I wanted control. Where did that get me? Into more heartache and trouble.

I often stood in a church service hearing salvation's call. While we stood singing "Just As I Am," I clenched my teeth and squeezed the church bench in front of me until my knuckles turned white.

The time and season came when You softened my heart and tenderly called me to Your throne of grace. I finally asked You to forgive my sins. I placed everything in Your hands. My sins, so many, took flight. A huge load lifted from my shoulders. Your Son, Jesus Christ, paid the price over 2,000 years ago so I could be set free. You forgave me, then cleansed and healed my wayward heart.

How wonderful and marvelous You are! Although I have sinned and come short of Your glory, You sent Your Son not to condemn but to save even me. You gave Your gift of an abundant, joy-filled, eternal life. Thank You, heavenly Father.

You are the Way, the Truth, the Life. I came to You through Your Son, Jesus Christ, and You adopted me as Your own.

Once I was lost. Now I am found. I was blind. Now I see. I give thanks to You, for You are God. I exalt Your holy name.

Learning to Forgive

Jan wheeled her red convertible into the hospital parking lot and rushed to the information desk. Her feet barely touched the hallway floors as she followed directions leading to the surgical waiting room. Thankful that Amanda's mother had called her, Jan greeted Amanda's parents with hugs and tears.

What had happened to Amanda? Her parents explained that Amanda had been riding too fast on her motorcycle. She had lost control on a curve and flown into gravel along the roadside. The doctors said Amanda wasn't critically injured but had a badly broken leg that required surgery.

Jan squeezed her eyes tightly as tears spilled. "I could have made a difference," she sobbed. "If only we had stayed close. I don't think I can forgive myself. She could have been killed."

Jan and Amanda had been friends since kindergarten. When the girls reached their late teens, however, their friendship changed. Unfriendly competition and put-downs damaged their mutual regard for each other. Jan listened to other so-called friends gossip about Amanda. Sadly, Jan believed their vile tales. Finally, the two young women went their separate ways.

Jan thought back to when she and Amanda were dedicated Christians, active in their church youth group. Now they avoided one another and never went to church.

Amanda's mother patted Jan's hand, as though she were reading the younger woman's mind. "Jan, you and Amanda have allowed needless things to separate you. If you take it all to the Lord and then each other, things will work out."

Jan wandered down to the hospital chapel and sat in an end pew. She drew her knees up to her chin, locked her arms around her legs, and looked up to the cross in front.

"I'm sorry, Lord," she whimpered. "I haven't been putting You first in my life. I want to be closer to You. Will You forgive me?

"Please help Amanda get well and show us how to forgive one another and restore our friendship."

Amanda's surgery was successful. She looked surprised and relieved when Jan came to visit. During the next few weeks, Jan went to see Amanda often. They shared their hurts and concerns honestly and talked for hours. They exposed and mended misunderstandings between them. They laughed and cried together. Jan and Amanda discovered they did not agree on everything, but they decided to agree to disagree and still be friends. God was teaching them how to love, forgive, and accept each other. God was also helping Jan forgive herself.

The best day in their friendship was when the two good friends returned to church—Amanda riding in a wheelchair, Jan pushing. Amanda and Jan and couldn't believe the sermon title in the church bulletin: FORGIVENESS.

Amanda leaned over to Jan. "We didn't just drift apart as friends," she whispered. "We drifted away from God and the church. He's been waiting for us here all along."

Jan smiled. "Let's start coming every Sunday and get on the right course."

They opened their songbooks and sang the familiar hymn "There's a Wideness in God's Mercy."

THERE'S A WIDENESS IN GOD'S MERCY

For the love of God is broader
Than the measure of our mind;
And the heart of the Eternal
Is most wonderfully kind.

FREDERICK WILLIAM FABER, 1854

Lord, I messed up again. Not only did I create stress in my own life, but I also hurt You and my relationship with others. How could I have been so uncaring and thoughtless? Please forgive me.

Hear my prayer, O Lord, for I need You more than life itself. Save me from these unkind things I have done and be compassionate to me. I cry to You with all my heart and lift my soul to Your loving presence. Give ear to me, O Lord; hear my earnest prayers. Listen to my supplications. In this day of my trouble, I beg for Your merciful forgiveness.

Thank You for Your boundless compassion. Though I feel unworthy, You are still here wrapping Your arms around me and loving me as Your wanted child. There is no other like You, dear Lord. Your wisdom and works exceed all else. I offer myself before You as a sacrifice. I worship You and want to glorify Your name. You alone are great and mighty. You alone are my God.

Help me let go of my stubborn ways. Cleanse my heart, I pray. Renew a pure spirit within me. Please grant me direction in righting the wrongs I have done. Give me strength, dear Lord, as I seek forgiveness from others. Even if I have been right in some ways, help me to let things go. Show me how to forgive no matter where the fault lies. Help me swallow my pride, even if others aren't willing to forgive or help to make things right.

I don't have the wisdom to straighten things out,
but I know You can show me, if I listen and obey You.
Instruct me, dear Lord, so I can follow Your upright
ways. Unite my heart with You as I glorify Your name
and praise You for Your merciful forgiveness.

FORGIVE AND FORGET

If I forgive, I must forget,
    Or forgive, I never shall do.
Forgiveness is like an unpaid bill
    Marked "Paid," then torn in two.

No matter the fault, the debt is gone.
    I never shall see it again.
Instead, I behold the old rugged cross,
    Where Jesus forgave my sin.

Take My Pride and Pain

Father, You know how much I hurt right now. I tried to make things right, but people simply don't always agree. Help me to forgive, even when I feel others are wrong. Remove my stubborn pride, Lord. Heal my pain. Comfort and restore others who are hurting. Help me surrender all to You and not take back anything.

I may not be able to do anything else at this time to solve this problem, but I know You can. Please be with those from whom I am distant. Remove all grudges, I pray. Bless and surround us with Your cleansing, forgiving Spirit. Grant us help to love and overlook the past as we press forward with You.

Do not repay anyone evil for evil. Be careful to do what is right in the eyes of everybody. If it is possible, as far as it depends on you, live at peace with everyone. Do not take revenge, my friends, but leave room for God's wrath, for it is written: "It is mine to avenge; I will repay," says the Lord. On the contrary:

"If your enemy is hungry, feed him; if he is thirsty, give him something to drink. In doing this, you will heap burning coals on his head."

Do not be overcome by evil, but overcome evil with good.

Romans 12:17–21 niv

Chapter 6

THANK YOU FOR
FAMILY AND FRIENDS

*Instead, be kind to each other,
tenderhearted, forgiving one another,
just as God has forgiven you because
you belong to Christ.*

EPHESIANS 4:32 TLB

*Don't just pretend that you love others:
really love them.*

ROMANS 12:9 TLB

Penned Friendship

After Shirley Green's husband died, she felt crushed and lonely. How could she manage? Shirley loved her grown children, but she needed friends, too. Now that she had retired from teaching, what could she do? She asked God to give her direction and fill her loneliness.

One afternoon, Shirley routinely checked her mail. "Water bill. Light bill," she murmured. "Some friends I have."

Beneath junk mail and bills, however, Shirley found a pink envelope. The return address showed that it was from Miami. She opened it curiously.

Dear Mrs. Green,

I'm Jennifer McCallan. You were my third-grade teacher. I hope this letter reaches you.

I live in Miami now and love my work as a model. I'm still not married, but I'm very happy. I have great friends and go to a wonderful church.

You showed me through your life what it meant to be a Christian. I just want to thank you.

Lately, I've been thinking of you and decided to write. Please write back when you can.

Sincerely,
Jennifer

P.S. Could you ever come to Miami for a visit?

Shirley felt like electricity went through the letter. Could this be her answered prayer? She wrote immediately and renewed their friendship. When Shirley added Jennifer's new address to her little book, she noticed lots of friends and family she could write to. After a short time, she had pen pals all over. Shirley's list grew, and her loneliness disappeared. She enjoyed visiting friends she had made, including Jennifer, throughout the United States and the world. When she was home, Shirley took as much pleasure in entertaining her friends in return.

Her pen pal list mushroomed to over fifty, but writing letters caused carpal tunnel syndrome to develop in her hands. With help from her family, Shirley purchased an electric typewriter. Her next step might be a computer and e-mail.

The awesome part of God's answer is how Shirley fills other people's loneliness. She gives a listening ear and comfort to many people. I wonder what Shirley will do next.

LONELINESS

He is a father to the fatherless; he gives justice to the widows, for he is holy. He gives families to the lonely.

PSALM 68:5–6 TLB

THANK YOU FOR THE ONE I MARRIED

Thank You for the one I married, Lord, and for the blessings You have bestowed upon us. It seems like yesterday when we stood before an altar and promised our lives to one another. Where have the years gone?

Thank You for teaching us to love, forgive, and love again. You are the head of our home. As we draw close to You, we automatically are united as one. I'm grateful for the many times we have combined our prayers for wisdom, love, and guidance; I thank You, too, for our children and grandchildren so dear. Thank You for being with us during the good times and for helping us when we face trials. Whenever either of us went through changes, we fell in love with each other again and again.

Bless us through our remaining years, dear Lord. Remind us to continue fanning the flame of love in our marriage, so it will always burn brightly with warmth and strength. May we grow old together, I pray. May he always bring me flowers. May I always bring a sparkle to his eyes.

Thank You for My Friends

Father, thank You for my true friends. They are the kind of friends who are there for me when things are right or when they go wrong. Thank You for the times they have gone out on a limb because they love and believe in me.

Help me, I pray, to be that kind of confidant and not be afraid to courageously stand up for them in all kinds of circumstances.

Unlimited Love

"My command is this: Love each other as I have loved you. Greater love has no one than this, that he lay down his life for his friends. You did not choose me, but I chose you and appointed you to go and bear fruit—fruit that will last. Then the Father will give you whatever you ask in my name. This is my command: Love each other."

John 15:12–13, 16–17 niv

The Argument

Linda sputtered at her husband, Don, and stormed out, angry enough to walk five miles. After a few blocks, her pace lessened. Her racing mind settled. She clutched her sweater with folded arms. Was she cold from the evening air or from the chilling words she had spoken? Did it really matter who was right or wrong? Linda thought of how defensive she'd become from her husband's comment. Could it be that there was some truth to what he'd said? She rounded another neighborhood block, afraid to apologize. What if he wouldn't listen? Must she state her view again?

Linda remembered the Bible verse: "Perfect love drives out fear" (1 John 4:18 NIV). Her conscience gently chided, *There is no need for excuses, just love.*

Her pace quickened, and Linda headed for home. When she approached their front yard, she could see the warm glow of living room lights. She quietly opened the door and paused, welcomed by Don's open arms. "I'm sorry," she cried.

"So am I."

"How could I have been so thoughtless?"

"We'll work it out."

"I'll try to understand."

The chill left. Love's warmth returned.

Lord, I did it again. I fell into another argument and spoke unkindly. Why was I so thoughtless? My heart feels heavy; I find myself replaying the disagreement all day. Can I be wrong although I know I'm "right"?

Is my attitude pure, unconditional love?

Please, calm my emotions. Help us to talk, to show respect, and to listen rather than argue.

When I must disagree, help me express my feelings with love, doing my best to keep this person's dignity intact. Show me how to separate the essential from the trivial and to know where I should give in. In spite of our differences, I must remain accepting of the one I love.

Has it been seventy times seven that I have forgiven? Help me show gentleness and forgiveness as You do. Let me be willing to not hold a grudge. Teach me to go beyond myself with thoughtfulness and kindness during this time, remembering that perfect love casts out fear.

Surround me and my loved one with Your presence and keep us nestled in Your pure, sweet love.

Keep Loving

Keep loving because of.
Keep loving in spite of.
Keep loving when to love is most difficult.
Keep loving when you have no strength.
Keep loving because Jesus loves you in good
    times and bad, on mountaintops, in valleys.
When all else fails, keep on loving.

A friend loveth at all times.

PROVERBS 17:17 KJV

Teach Me to Parent

Thank You for my children, Lord. They are my most precious gifts from You. I look at them and see how they reflect different family members—their hair, their eyes, the little dimple like mine. Most of all, I pray they will have Your eyes and learn the wonders of Your ways.

Help me teach my children the lessons in Your Word. Remind me to talk about Your scriptures in our home. May this become a way of life. Through the years, I pray my dear ones will learn to apply Your lessons to all they do.

When I must discipline, grant me love, strength, and consistency. Let me lead them into a life of love, responsibility, truth, and hope for the future. Grant me understanding as I work with each child, so I won't be too strict nor too lenient. Help me develop love and security in them, rather than fear and anger. Let everything I do be out of loving action, not reaction.

I can't think of a job more challenging than meeting the needs of my children. I can only do it through You, my Lord. Go before me, I pray. As I endeavor to do Your will, I petition Your help. Enable me to train up my children in the way they should go, so when they are older, they will remain close to You. In Jesus' name, I pray, amen.

Blest Be the Tie That Binds

Before our Father's throne
We pour our ardent prayers;
Our fears, our hopes, our aims are one
Our comforts and our cares.

JOHN FAWCETT, 1782

*"And these words which I command you today shall
be in your heart. You shall teach them diligently to
your children, and shall talk of them when you sit
in your house, when you walk by the way, when
you lie down, and when you rise up. You shall bind
them as a sign on your hand, and they shall be as
frontlets between your eyes. You shall write them
on the doorposts of your house and on your gates."*

DEUTERONOMY 6:6–9 NKJV

CALLED APART

Greg and Myrna lived in a happy Christian home filled with teenagers. All were active in the church, with Greg leading singing and serving on the church board and Myrna teaching Sunday school.

As time went on, things changed. Their children chose different standards for themselves, and God no longer remained their priority or interest. The teenagers were making decisions in their lives that could be disastrous.

Friction replaced joy in their home. Greg and Myrna struggled to work things out but couldn't keep afloat. How could they be Christian leaders when things weren't right at home?

The brokenhearted couple came to the Lord for direction. Because they wanted to put more love and energy into their children, Greg and Myrna both cut back on their church responsibilities. But doing less in the church was a big adjustment. A wise Christian friend sensed their need and wrote the following letter:

> *Dear Greg and Myrna,*
>
> *I have been praying for you today and felt God lead me to share some lessons I learned while we were raising our teenagers.*
>
> *First, you are doing the right thing by obeying God as He calls you apart. This is the time to focus your whole hearts and souls on your children. They are your most precious commodities.*
>
> *Second, raising a family isn't always a bed of*

roses. When we brought these children into this world, they came with their own minds and wills.

Third, you are not alone. Sometimes we as Christians try to appear happy-go-lucky to one another rather than sharing our needs. Some people may turn their backs on you, but you really do have friends who love you and care. A few of us walked this road before you.

Fourth, when the struggles hit close to home, keep loving, forgiving, and praying. Cling tightly to Jesus, the blessed vine. He is your source of nourishment and strength. When you are discouraged, God will truly hold you up.

Fifth, the more you pray and keep loving, the stronger you will become. God will teach you some wonderful lessons through this. The only way you make it through is by spending earnest time in your prayer closet.

Sixth, thank God for your kids every day. When they do the smallest good things, tell them you are proud of them, that you love and appreciate them. Forgive them when they mess up. Try to love, understand, and accept them right where they are. Look for their strengths. Tell them you believe in them and know they will become fine Christian adults. Never fear, God is right there with them.

Seventh, after you make it through the crisis, you will all look back and thank God for the miracles! When the victories are won, remember to pass on your love and blessings to other parents.

I love you all and am here for you,
Marlene

Greg and Myrna made their share of mistakes along the way, but they kept loving and praying for their children.

And God did perform miracles. Now the entire family thanks God for how He brought them through the tough times. Every one of Greg and Myrna's children loves the Lord and is a responsible adult.

The Christian couple is grateful to God that He called them apart to focus on the ones most important to them, their own family. Now they have the chance to help others and share the lessons they learned.

Thank You for Loving My Children

Father, these are frightening times for me, but I trust my children to Your care. Thank You for loving and helping them.

Grant me patience to love, wisdom to understand, and grace to accept them. I know You are watching over them, so I will not fear. I believe in my children because I see the good in them.

Thank You for calling me apart and guiding me through. I already praise You for answered prayers to come.

In Jesus' name, amen.

Learning to Let Go

Dear Father, I have done all I can to help. Yet I see my loved one's unwise decisions. I know I need to let go, but my love makes it impossible. Are You teaching me that by letting go I can show even greater love?

I realize my helplessness in solving another's problems. So, Lord, I place this one of mine in Your hands. I know You love each of us more than we can imagine. My dear one is no exception.

Grant me strength to stand up for what is right but to keep on loving. When unkind remarks hurt, let me not turn away but merely step aside and give some space. Help me not to take the problems back by manipulating, fixing, or condemning, but to lend words of encouragement.

Teach me to be a comforter, not a crutch; to care, not to control; to listen, not demand my own way; and to cherish the good moments of each day.

I will not grieve for the past but will look to the future in hopeful anticipation.

Father, thank You for taking my fear and replacing it with Your pure love. Protect us with Your angels and guide us with Your Spirit, that we will not fall to evil and harm.

My Friend

What a wonderful gift You have given me, Father, in my dear friend. Thank You for her! In good times and bad she is there. She is a loving friend when I am at my best or my worst. In adversity, she is loyal. She rejoices with me in my gladness. She sheds tears and prays for me in my sorrows. I am so grateful for her, Lord.

Thank You for how You gave me my friend. It happened as though You planned it all along. I rejoice that she needs me, too. Thank You for showing me how to be kind and compassionate and alert to my friend's concerns and needs. When we get together, I talk and she listens; then she talks and I listen.

When I err, thank You for her forgiveness. When I do things right, thank You for her smile. She is a friend I can share my deepest secrets with. Hers are buried deep within my well of prayers, not to be revealed to anyone other than You. I praise You, Lord, for my friend, my sister in Christ.

And let us consider how we may spur one another on toward love and good deeds. Let us not give up meeting together, as some are in the habit of doing, but let us encourage one another.

Hebrews 10:24–25 niv

Chapter 7

THANK YOU FOR YOUR CHURCH

Consequently, you are no longer foreigners and aliens, but fellow citizens with God's people and members of God's household, built on the foundation of the apostles and prophets, with Christ Jesus himself as the chief cornerstone. In him the whole building is joined together and rises to become a holy temple in the Lord. And in him you too are being built together to become a dwelling in which God lives by his Spirit.

EPHESIANS 2:19–22 NIV

He [Jesus] told them, "The harvest is plentiful, but the workers are few. Ask the Lord of the harvest, therefore, to send out workers into his harvest field."

LUKE 10:2 NIV

Hear the Call

I hear Jesus call to me,
  "There's work for you to do."
I see many hurting souls.
  "Come, show them life anew."

"You must reap the harvest,
  Of those who search for Me."
I still hear Him calling:
  "From sin, I'll set them free."

God, why must I be the one?
  Why are You calling *me*?
"Because they need *your* help, My child."
  Then here am I, send me.

*How, then, can they call on the one they
have not believed in? And how can they
believe in the one of whom they have not
heard? And how can they hear without
someone preaching to them? And how can
they preach unless they are sent? As it is
written, "How beautiful are the feet of
those who bring good news!"*

ROMANS 10:14–15 NIV

Building the Future with God

The first Sunday Stacy and Karen Scott arrived to pastor a local church, Bob and I wouldn't have missed it for anything in the world. Stacy wore the same brush haircut and broad grin he had twenty years before. Karen looked lovely and not a year older. It was as if the couple was returning home.

Twenty years before, Stacy and Karen had served as dedicated youth pastors in the same church. They had spent countless hours spiritually nurturing our teenage sons, as well as some twenty other young people. No one wanted to see them leave, but God was calling them to a different location.

Now, on their return, Stacy and Karen are able to enjoy the fruits of their past years' work. A new generation has arrived. Youth who once learned from Stacy and Karen are now adults with families of their own, filling the same pews, serving on church committees and boards, and singing to the glory of God. Church altars are filled. People are growing in the Lord!

Stacy and Karen have a gratifying opportunity once again to affect the future of the church through the present and upcoming generations.

Thank God for those who hear His call and faithfully follow year after year—touching lives, winning souls, and helping to build the future with God!

Lighting Our World

A certain man's life story recently made the national news.

After more than twenty years as a teacher and municipal planner, this man heard God's call to study for the ministry. So he entered theological seminary and began taking classes, mostly by correspondence.

His day usually began at five in the morning with homework and extra study, followed by his daily school routine. After several years, he completed his academic requirements, graduated from seminary, and was ordained a minister.

But his ministry was as different as his path to seminary. He felt God's call to become a chaplain for senior citizens and to preach in local churches when pastors were absent.

His zeal and enthusiasm for life has become an inspiration to many. In addition to his duties, he reads voraciously, enjoys writing, and plays hymns on his keyboard.

But what is so special about this man that merited mention on the news? When he began his studies in seminary four years ago, he was over ninety years old! In spite of his age—or because of it—he is still obeying God's new challenges to reach souls for Christ and help light our world.

A Rare Jewel

I proudly gazed at sixteen-year-old Michelle as she once again helped a group of our Sunday school children memorize Bible verses. Her long, blond hair fell softly forward when she bent close with a listening ear. A shy little girl with clasped hands behind her back whispered her newly learned verse. Afterward, Michelle praised her for a job well-done.

The first time I met Michelle was when she started coming to our church about two years ago. I thought at the time she had something special about her. I almost could see LEADERSHIP printed right across her forehead.

It wasn't long until Michelle accepted my invitation to help me in Bible Explorer's Club. The program is built on individualized Bible memorization, so I'm always grateful for assistance.

I was delighted to discover that Michelle had studied the same program as a child. She jumped right in like it was second nature.

Last Christmas, Michelle accepted the job of directing our children's Christmas program. She rewrote the script, recruited faithful helpers, and produced a successful program for us all to enjoy.

Michelle has many wonderful abilities far beyond her years. But the one that shines above them all is her commitment to faithfulness. We have all seen people who possess the abilities—but if you can't depend on them, none of that matters. Keeping a promise is important to Michelle, a marvelous attribute for a teenage girl.

She is a rare jewel. I love her and appreciate her. I wish I could keep her forever. Thank you, Michelle, for your faithfulness.

Gift of Helps

It was the end of a typical worship service. I happened to glance across the sanctuary just in time to see Jan do one more good turn for someone. How did she seem to know just the right thing to do? The answer was simple.

Jan has a way of tuning in to God's call and responding with every ounce of strength she can muster. Constantly on the lookout, she is extremely sensitive to the needs of those around her.

The most wonderful part is that Jan doesn't appear to be interested in receiving any recognition for the things she does. She merely renders help, puts it behind her, and goes on.

Jan looks for the best in everyone she meets. When she comes to the aid of others, there are no strings attached. She doesn't want them to feel obligated, nor does she try to run their lives. She simply loves and cares. She makes no big deal but smiles as though helping and giving warms her heart.

Quiet, thoughtful acts often have a way of multiplying in value. They range from kind notes sent to someone, groceries or money given to those in need, and pinch-hitting for different church committees, to slipping coloring pages and crayons to a restless child in church.

Where does she get this talent? God blesses some folks with numerous gifts of the Holy Spirit, as mentioned in 1 Corinthians 12, and upon some Christians, He bestows the gift of helps. The gift of helps unselfishly uses all the productive *fruit* of God's Holy Spirit: unconditional love; overflowing joy; peace that surpasses all understanding; enduring patience; tireless kindness; unselfish goodness; faithfulness in all circumstances; empathizing gentleness; and strong, steady self-control.

How beautiful it is when someone with God's gift of helps hardly ever notices when others fail and *forgets* his or her personal loving deeds given!

Thank you, Jan, for blessing those around you with God's gift of helps.

> *Be of the same mind toward one another.*
> *Do not set your mind on high things, but*
> *associate with the humble. Do not be wise*
> *in your own opinion.*

> ROMANS 12:16 NKJV

Your Church

For Your church, my heavenly Father, I thank You. Thank You for founding it, for purchasing it with the blood of Your Son, Jesus Christ. Not a building, but a courageous body of believers who through the years have given their all to be able to worship You. Your church has persevered during wars, tribulations, bountiful blessings, and heartbreaking failures.

For the love of Jesus that has bound Your church body together through the ages, I praise You. For those who bravely stepped forward; accepted Him as their Savior; were cleansed, baptized, and went on to give a lifetime of service to You; I thank You.

Although riddled with arrows from the evil one, Your church stands. When razor-sharp tongues attempt to amputate parts of its precious body, it still remains and comes back stronger than ever as we trust in and obey You.

As I watch on our day of worship, I see many people who mean so much: the custodians; those who bring flowers; others involved with refreshments; the organizers, donators, youth, and children; the parents, elders, music groups, pastors, and pastors' wives; the missionaries; and (bless their hearts) the prayer warriors. The list goes on and on. When one isn't in church, there's a gap. No one in Your family is less or more important than any other. Each one matters to You, and I thank You for them.

Thank You for asking me to be part of Your church. I praise You for giving us the ability to love and give to one another. When one is happy, we all rejoice. When another is hurting, we hurt with them, pray for them, and help them. Little by little, we are learning to become soul winners. Thank You for helping us to constantly reach out and invite new people into Your family.

In light of Your presence, I am grateful for these, my dear family of God, who care about and love me. The bond we share may or may not be biological. It is one that is sealed by the blood of Your Son, Jesus Christ. Thank You for how You provide the same power that raised Jesus from the dead and gave us eternal life to protect, care for, and increase this holy church throughout the ages.

Let the filling of Your cleansing Holy Spirit within this church begin within my heart. May all we say and do please and glorify You. Praise be to You, my heavenly Father, for Your church.

CHRISTIAN LOVE

Lonely hearts long for love,
    While each day rushes by.
Weary souls have no love,
    Yet each day rushes by.
Take a smile, pass it on,
    When you go hurrying by.
Say a prayer, do a deed,
    For each day rushes by.

Grandma's Lamp

Weather back in Mizpah, Montana, during the winter is so cold sometimes it isn't fit for man or beast. That was the case during a brutal winter in 1937.

Dad was only eighteen. Although the weather was bad, his brother Bill still carried on his job doing roadwork about four or five miles from their home. Dad was planning to ride his horse, Coon, out to check on Bill, then return home.

Dad knew he wouldn't make it home before dark. Everything grew pitch-black when night fell. There were no streetlights. Country folks didn't have electricity back then. Neighbors lived miles apart.

To make things worse, snow began flying and drifting like crazy. Dad's mother was concerned about him getting lost in the storm. She told him she would place a kerosene lamp in the window for him. The home place sat at the end of their mile-long private road. A lamp could be plainly seen from a long distance.

Dad reached Bill, saw he was all right, and dropped off some food. Dark, lowering clouds made nightfall come fast. Things couldn't have been blacker. No moon. No stars. Snow flurries worsened and drifted so high, not a fence post could be found. The usual emerald trees crowned with snow didn't break the darkness.

In spite of the elements, Dad wasn't worried. His horse was one of the best. Coon bent his head low while Dad hunched over his back. Icy winds whistled hollow, mournful songs and tore at Coon and at Dad's clothing as they pressed toward home.

Dad recalls how bad it was: "It was dark all right, when I was headin' home. Pitch-black, it was. Just inky black sky 'n cuttin' wind 'n white snow everywhere."

After riding a few miles, Dad finally spotted a shaft of light from the lamp his mother had placed in the window. Nothing to worry about. Dad confidently kept riding in the direction of the light. He looked forward to getting home, safe and warm.

But something was wrong. The light moved! Wasn't it the lamp? He wondered if the light came from a passing car, traveling on the other side of the river.

It was plain to Dad that he had lost his bearings. Getting turned around was way too dangerous in such weather, especially at night. He studied the situation. Who had the most sense at this point? He? Or the horse? It didn't take long for Dad to decide.

He dropped the reins, let them rest on the saddle horn, and gave Coon his head. Dad knew his horse could bring them safely home.

Coon did just that. Before long, rider and horse worked their way down the mile-long road to the house.

After he got the horse settled in the barn and went inside the house, Dad found out what had been wrong. While he was watching the lamp, his mother moved it from one window to another to make it more visible.

Think for a moment of our spiritual lights being like Grandma's lamp. We may already be letting our lights shine for those around us the way God wants us to do. But we must be careful to remain consistent and dependable in our walk with the Lord. Others are watching and counting on us to lead the way. Let's set a straight course as we walk our spiritual walk, so they can see a good example. In this way, the light we are shining will lead them straight to the heavenly Father.

> "You are the light of the world.
> A city that is set on a hill cannot be hidden.
> Nor do they light a lamp
> and put it under a basket,
> but on a lampstand,
> and it gives light to all who are in the house.
> Let your light so shine before men,
> that they may see your good works
> and glorify your Father in heaven."
>
> MATTHEW 5:14–16 NKJV

Chapter 8

THANK YOU FOR GROWING ME

"Take my yoke upon you and learn from me, for I am gentle and humble in heart, and you will find rest for your souls. For my yoke is easy and my burden is light."

MATTHEW 11:28–30 NIV

The things which you learned and received and heard and saw in me, these do, and the God of peace will be with you.

PHILIPPIANS 4:9 NKJV

The Potter

Lord, it makes no difference what comes my way. What really matters is for me to be within Your will. Help me become soft and pliable, so You can mold me the way You know I should be.

The potter's wheel spins round and round. Gentle fingers form the soft clay into the master's desired creation. To the potter, there is purpose in each turn.

At times, my life seems to be spinning. Slow me down, Lord. You are the Potter of my life. Let me heed to Your molding so I can be a product of Your perfect plan.

Does not the potter have the right
to make out of the same lump of clay
some pottery for noble purposes and
some for common use?

ROMANS 9:21 NIV

Teach Me Self-Control

Father, thank You for teaching me to think before I speak or act. I know sometimes it's difficult for You to get me to listen. I praise You for how Your Holy Spirit warns me against serious mistakes. The words in Your Bible grant me wisdom and remind me to exercise self-control. May everything I say and do show kindness and love to others.

O Master, Let Me Walk with Thee

O Master, let me walk with Thee,
In lowly paths of service free;
Tell me Thy secret; help me bear
The strain of toil, the fret of care.

Help me the slow of heart to move
By some clear, winning word of love;
Teach me the wayward feet to stay,
And guide them in the homeward way.

Teach me Thy patience; still with Thee
In closer, dearer company,
In work that keeps faith sweet and strong,
In trust that triumphs over wrong.

Washington Gladden, 1879

Thank You for the Man I Love

He gazes at me from across the packed room. We're at just another meeting, but I dressed to look my best. Do I see the same twinkle in his eyes I saw when we first met? Do I see the same look he wore on our wedding day? Am I so blessed that he still gazes at me with the same love and pride? Thank You, Lord, for that look. Thank You for today and for him.

Help me show to him the same love and thoughtfulness as when we were first married. In our hurried schedules, let us look for time to spend with each other. Sometimes I love even sharing a second glass of iced tea on the patio at sundown.

I think of changes we've faced and will continue to experience. We have fallen in love with each other over and over again, even while changing.

Teach us to keep respecting one another's feelings. Teach us to put each other first, after You.

And, Lord, help me keep myself in a way that he will always look across the room with love and pride.

And now these three remain:
faith, hope and love.
But the greatest of these is love.

1 Corinthians 13:13 niv

Press On

Press on thro' strong temptation,
For Satan's hosts must flee;
In Jesus' name, resist them
And vict'ry thine shall be.

B. ELLIOTT WARREN, 1897

I Focus on You

Though temptations surround me on every side, I keep my focus on You. I know You are far greater than any traps set in my way.

The devil often tempts me in my weakest areas. When this happens, I refuse to dwell on the temptation. Instead, I give the problem to You, Lord. Whatever temptations I face, others have encountered before me. I trust You to take them all, making a way for me to escape and be victorious in You.

Let me look directly ahead and focus on You, my Lord. Keep my way straight and level, my faith firmly planted in You. Thank You for leading and helping me every step of the way.

TEMPTATION

Let your eyes look straight ahead, fix your gaze directly before you. Make level paths for your feet and take only ways that are firm. Do not swerve to the right or the left; keep your foot from evil.

PROVERBS 4:25–27 NIV

LOOKING STRAIGHT AHEAD

My husband, Bob, recently took up walking three miles every other day in order to lose some weight and shape up. I decided several weeks later to join him on his walk through town.

While we trekked down Main Street, Bob shared a valuable lesson with me. He said walking was not the hard part. The challenge was passing the pizza shop, a hot dog stand, the doughnut store, two deli shops, and an ice cream parlor.

I thought a lot about Bob's story in relation to our walks with God. It isn't our step with God that's difficult; it's our walking (or running) straight forward, past the temptations along the way. We can do so only by focusing on Him.

Moving a Mountain
a Teaspoonful at a Time

This mountain of mine is huge, Father! I've prayed over and over that You would remove it from me, but still it remains, looming, threatening. Must I move it myself? I don't think I can handle such a task.

There's much to be done and so little time. Yet I am determined. Whether I'm weary or not, in season or out, I must begin moving my mountain, even if it's only a teaspoonful at a time.

Lord, help me face each problem head-on within Your will. When fires and hot, parching winds surround me, remind me You are here. When fierce storms assault me, help me dig in my heels and hang on to Your Word. When I'm forced to plod through sinful murk and mud, I ask You to cleanse me with Your pure, sweet living water. Lighten my step that I don't get bogged down in such things.

When evil seeks to devour me, I seek protection with Your holy armor. When others criticize me and self-righteously smirk at my mountain, I may feel crushed and defeated. Lift me up then, I pray. Help me hold my head high and go on. For I am Your child—the child of the King!

When life's heavy trees and rocks fall on and about me, I shall not fear, for You are helping, guiding all the way.

At times, I may ask, "Why me, Lord? Why must I move this mountain and carry this tree, my cross? I'm too weak!" Please help me. Please love me. I trust

You, for this mountain shall be removed, and I praise You for the victories to come.

> *Jesus looked at them and said,*
> *"With man this is impossible,*
> *but with God all things are possible."*
>
> MATTHEW 19:26 NIV

Wouldn't it be wonderful if we could call on God and He would snap His gingers and make all our troubles disappear? It rarely works that way.

I'm reminded of how God works these things together for a purpose. I watch athletes train day after weary day, building their strength, preparing for competition. How proud they are of their improvements! I think of students who toil long and hard for degrees, or artists who paint landscapes, starting over and over until they're right.

What about disasters? Many thrown our way loom like mountains, but with God's help we can work through them all. Each time, we grow. We feel pride, strength, and satisfaction that we could never have experienced if all were handed to us on a silver platter.

There are reasons God lets us struggle. There are lessons to learn and lives to touch along the way. At times our mountains prepare us to help others.

When I watch the ants, I'm awed at the huge loads they carry, some far bigger than their bodies. They never give up, but keep struggling. When the load is too great, another ant often shows up. I wish

I could reach down to help but I'm too big. Perhaps that's why God sends other Christians to help us. May they not idly stand by or criticize. God is working when another dear one picks up a teaspoon and pitches in.

The day comes when we look back at what we have accomplished with God's help in moving that mountain and carrying our cross. We can see ruts and furrows along the way. Where did they come from? Surely we weren't strong enough to make them! Some have come from His almighty hand —some were made when Jesus picked up our heavy cross and carried it for us.

You Said I Could Do It

Some said I couldn't do it.
Some shook their heads in doubt.
Some rolled their eyes and sighed.
"You can never work it out."

You said I could do it:
The task You gave to me.
I worked from dawn through dusk,
With help that came from Thee.

And now that it's complete,
New goals You place ahead.
I'm glad I showed You honor,
And heard Your voice instead.

———❧———

Ignore the doubter.
    Remain strong.
Don't be afraid to fail.
    Keep your eye on the goal.
Maintain a realistic pace.
    Listen to the One who coaches you.

My son, keep your father's commands and do not forsake your mother's teaching. Bind them upon your heart forever; fasten them around your neck.

When you walk, they will guide you; when you sleep, they will watch over you; when you awake, they will speak to you.

For these commands are a lamp, this teaching is a light, and the corrections of discipline are the way to life.

PROVERBS 6:20–23 NIV

Therefore, since we are surrounded by
such a great cloud of witnesses,
let us throw off everything that hinders
and the sin that so easily entangles,
and let us run with perseverance
the race marked out for us.

HEBREWS 12:1 NIV

You Are First and Last

As I look back on my life, Father, I marvel at the mighty ways Your hand has been upon me. Before I was born, You formed me and watched over me. In my childhood, You were there. When I asked You into my heart, You blessed me. Through my bumpy teenage years, You rescued me from wrong circumstances. Now I am an adult. You still are with me, helping and guiding me all the way.

Though my life is changing all the time, I shall not fear. The past was in Your hands; so do I place the future. You are my Lord. You are my beginning, my present, my future, and my eternity.

When times are difficult and my soul feels dry, I know You are here—pouring out Your Holy Spirit upon me. When all is well, You still remain—counseling, leading me all the way.

Bestow Your call to not only use my life, Lord, but those of my offspring. Keep them close to You. Protect them from wrongdoing and harm. May they, too, glorify You. Teach them the marvelous lessons You show to me. Let them spring up like grass in the field—like sturdy poplar trees, growing by flowing streams.

I pray they will always say, "I belong to the Lord. He is my all in all."

Passing the Test

I felt tested to the limit, Lord, but through it all, I knew You were there, helping, strengthening, and comforting me. I don't know why I had to struggle; but You knew the answers, and I trusted You. In the fiery trials, I still put my confidence in You and obeyed. I know You and love You, my Lord.

You refined me like a precious metal. You stood nearby and watched while my impurities painfully burned away. Now, I pray, allow me to offer You a pure heart as a sacrifice of praise and thanksgiving.

Should I be required to go through further fiery afflictions, I know I will not be consumed. Your compassionate Holy Spirit will go with me. You will give me strength to pass the test, and I will praise You again.

For you, O God, tested us;
*   you refined us like silver.*
You brought us into prison
*   and laid burdens on our backs.*
You let men ride over our heads;
*   we went through fire and water,*
but you brought us to a place of abundance.
Praise be to God, who has not rejected my
prayer or withheld his love from me!

Psalm 66:10–12, 20 niv

All You Have Done

You have led me through so many wildernesses in my life, Father. Sometimes I even needed forty years, like Moses, to find my way out. Oh, the testing and trials along the way. The darkness, the storms, the frightening shadows, and the fears for the future. At times, I couldn't see my way. Would the sun ever shine again? The struggles reduced my spirit to humiliation, defeat, and nothingness. I couldn't see the point of it all, only the agony. But You could.

When I had nowhere to go, I finally started to obey You, my heavenly Father. Thank You for walking by and finding me along the wilderness path. Your directions were right, Your lessons true. Even the trials taught me wisdom and made me strong.

Once, when things were easy, I had become careless. But the trials caused me to cling to You, Father.

I don't know how I made it through each wilderness, except for all You did to help me. Somehow the miracles of time and circumstance fell into place.

You are a dear Father to me, understanding and caring. You took a little person like me, struggling along the wilderness way. You tended, fed, and watered me until I came into full bloom for Your glory. Then You brought me out to the other side where the sun shone brightly again. Thank You for all You have done.

Chapter 9

THANK YOU FOR GUIDING ME

You give me your shield of victory,
and your right hand sustains me;
you stoop down to make me great.
You broaden the path beneath me,
so that my ankles do not turn.

PSALM 18:35–36 NIV

Thou shalt guide me with thy counsel, and
afterward receive me to glory.

PSALM 73:24 KJV

Take the Controls, Lord

Life is out of control right now, Lord. Things are pretty frightening. I want to panic and bail out. Instead, I call on Your help.

Take the controls of my life, Lord. You can change chaos and fear into Your divine order. In quietness and confidence, I draw my strength from You. As You take the controls, I will rest and trust in Your wisdom and mighty power to guide me through.

He Holds My Hand

Dangers surround me, and dark is the way,
But Jesus leadeth me.
He is my strength for the long weary day,
No matter what may be.

NORMAN J. CLAYTON, 1938

I Look to You, Dear Lord

You are my hope, the Lord of my life. I wait on You and move cautiously in my decisions. I'm not ashamed to trust in Your guidance, Lord. Instead, I feel thankful for the encouragement and surety You give me. As I trust in You, I'm filled with peace. Throughout the day, my thoughts often turn to You for direction and strength. In quiet and confidence, I find the strength only You can give.

You, dear Father, are my Rock and my Defender; I shall not fear. I know in whom I believe, and I'm persuaded You keep me close to You day by day.

I look to You; I doubt not in Your unfailing love for me. Thank You.

In Jesus' name, amen.

Moving Forward with You

In You, I put my trust and hope, Lord God, for You are the One who holds my future. Thank You for the plans You have for me. I may shake in my boots, but I will still move forward and obey Your will. I behold Your presence as You gaze upon my transparent soul. You know me well and can see far better than I the best ways for me to go.

I look up with steadfast trust and thank You for how Your mercy and love surround me. I praise You for helping me to move forward with You.

BOLDNESS TO DO RIGHT

Boldness from God is
    to fear not when giving your all;
    to shun not when risking for Christ;
    to shrink not when standing for right;
    to waver not in honesty and integrity;
    to limit not the capacity to love;
    to squelch not enthusiasm for Christ;
    to seek not the limelight lest you fall and;
    to heed not those who speak wrong.

God's Holy Spirit helps us
    be bold for the truth in His Spirit;
    be bold to serve Christ in His Spirit and;
    be bold to tell of God's love in His Spirit.

In so doing, we shall be carried by the power of God over the deepest and most treacherous of life's challenges.

Mark loved his church's adult class. The group often became engaged in lively discussions. Best of all, his teacher challenged the group in their walk with God to make it an everyday experience.

Recently, the class began learning how God could guide them if they would tune in and obey. The teacher passed out devotional books to the group and encouraged them to read a little each day.

"You need to start with prayer; then read your Bible and devotional book every day possible," the teacher announced.

Mark felt this sounded great. He decided to begin immediately. The next morning, he awakened a little earlier to take time with God. Mark enjoyed this time, but he felt no special direction from God. The next week, Mark told the class what happened. He wanted God to guide him.

Again, the teacher challenged Mark and the class. "The next step is to remember communication with God needs to go both ways. After you finish praying and reading your Bible, listen with your mind and your heart. You'll be surprised at how God works."

The following morning, Mark did exactly as the teacher said. Before long, he felt a guiding Presence. Mark questioned God about different things in his life. He listened for answers. He wanted God to use him more than anything.

When Mark prepared to leave for work one morning, he grabbed his briefcase and newspaper.

He always read on the bus. The church devotional book on the coffee table loomed up at him. This time he felt God urging him to take it along.

For the rest of the week, Mark obeyed God's lead. Not only did he read a page from the small book, he tore the sheet out and left it on the seat before leaving the bus. He continued doing the same thing every day.

"What's so exciting about this?" Mark murmured under his breath.

Tom lived close to town. His fiancée had recently died from a serious heart condition. Tom tried helping with her medical bills. He could barely make ends meet with his current job. Tom was so distraught he felt like taking his own life. He wondered if there was a God up there who even cared.

Each day, Tom boarded the same bus where Mark stepped off. They nodded, barely noticing one another.

One Wednesday, Tom boarded the bus. He and Mark happened to sit in the same spot. Tom noticed the paper on the seat. He picked it up and began reading mindlessly. It didn't take long before Tom became interested in the stories.

Weeks went by. Mark kept faithfully reading the devotions on the way to work, Tom finding them on the seat.

Mark continued wondering about God's leading.

Was God really guiding him, or had it been Mark's imagination all along?

Tom started watching for the papers. His attitude toward life was taking a new turn. He wondered if God really did care about him. Maybe there was something to becoming a Christian.

One day, Mark's work required him to make his first stop at another business farther into town, so he remained on the bus.

Tom climbed on the bus and sat across from Mark. Neither noticed the other. Mark finished the daily reading, tore it out, and placed it on the seat beside him.

"You're the one!" Tom exclaimed. "I've been reading these papers every day. They are giving me hope to go on."

Mark stared with amazement as Tom briefly told him about his fiancée and the hard times. A warm feeling grew inside Mark. He was beginning to understand God's remarkable communication and work.

"Let's get together and talk," Mark urged. "How about one night after work this week?"

Tom agreed wholeheartedly.

Soon after, Tom started going with Mark to the church adult class. Mark also helped Tom find a better job in Mark's company. The two became good friends.

GUIDE

Be Thou my guide,
Through life's treacherous way.
Be Thou my rock,
On it will I stay.

Be Thou my might;
Grant me strength anew.
Be Thou my map;
Gently lead me through.

Be Thou my song,
So I will not fear.
Be Thou my stay;
Keep me safe and near.

Be Thou my grace;
Firmly clasp my hand.
Be Thou my guide,
To the promised land.

Small shells crunched into the pebbled sand beneath Rose's feet as she walked the Jamestown beach. Her legs felt weighted down after trudging only a few miles.

Rose sat on a log and gazed across the water. The sound looked as calm as a lake. The outgoing tide revealed a small spit where seagulls rested in partial sunlight. It was so quiet Rose could hear boat motors from miles away and an occasional passing car from the street behind her.

The tide was out, making it possible for blue herons to elegantly stand in shallow water a safe distance from shore. How she would love to see them fly. Winds blowing the tide, creating ripples, caused the sea life to continually adjust to nature's rhythm. Rose breathed deeply and filled her lungs with the clean, salty air.

A purple-shaded mountain range surrounded most of the area as far as she could see. To her left, the long Dungeness Spit stretched its huge finger out into the water for about twelve miles. She pulled out her binoculars to get a better look. Near the end of the spit, she could see a well-kept lighthouse. Its white paint and red trim shone brightly in the sun, in contrast to the surrounding blue sky and water.

Rose stirred the toe of her tennis shoe in the sand. The beachfront was changing as she sat there. She had been told when the storms come in the strong waves could move ten-foot logs up and down the beach. Rose thought of the changes she, too, was constantly facing. Like the sea life, she had to continually develop a rhythm through wavering ups and downs and readjustments, while God's constant, gentle leading rippled through her everyday life—cleansing, shifting, and refreshing her.

Rose reached into her backpack and pulled out her journal, pen, and small Bible. They went almost everywhere with her like best friends. She began to read: "To everything there is a season, a time for every purpose under heaven" (Ecclesiastes 3:1 NKJV).

As Rose read some of her journal's log of events from her life, she could clearly see God's hand at work. She read about prayers being answered during the ups and downs through the past years. Monstrous problems had been solved. Huge splinters that felt as big as the seashore logs had been removed. Sometimes Rose had felt battered by troubles and wondered if she would survive. But now she could see how God's finger had created a long protecting bulwark for her, buffering her from harsh storms.

In her darkest hours, when she thought she would crash against the rocks, the lighthouse of God's Word had helped her find the way. When pressures fogged her thinking and she didn't know which way to turn, she remembered His speaking to her heart. Like a foghorn cutting through the murky air, God's unmistakable voice had cut through uncertainties.

Rose turned to a clean page in her journal and

began writing: "I don't know what the future holds, Lord, but I know You are here every step of the way. Guarding. Guiding. Keeping."

YOU ARE MY GLIMMER OF HOPE

When everything seems hopeless, You are my glimmer of hope, Lord. I will trust in You with all my heart. You are my light and my salvation. I know I won't remain in darkness when I follow You. Thank You for how Your light and mine will shine wherever we go.

WELL-WORN PATH

The path Jesus leads us on isn't meant to be taken only once.

We reach the glorious decision to follow Him, and our spirits soar. We digest the Bible's teachings like tasty life-giving morsels of bread. We experience His blessings and drink of His cleansing fountain. But a piece of bread, a drink of water, and rest for the body only strengthen us for one day. In the same way, Jesus wants us to fortify our souls and minds when we come to Him in prayer again and again. Only then do we remain strong Christians.

God wants us to read our Bibles and pray often. Each time we do, the Savior provides us with spiritual energy that recharges us to go on. After we rise from our knees, we are able to follow the hem of His robe again.

Every day is a brand-new adventure with God. Each one begins with His starting us on the holy path once more, aligned with His will. Spending time in prayer becomes a way of life.

It's never too soon or too late to begin following the path God has for you. Choose it soon. Feel His strength and glory. Enjoy reading His words in your Bible. See what a wonderful life He has in the making for you.

After you have tried this path with Jesus for a while and made it a way of life, you will look back on your well-worn trail and see how it has become the best road you could have ever taken: a life that's free, filled with joy and victory.

How Priceless You Are

You are so dear to me, Lord, while we walk this path of life together. How priceless You are to me. You are my way of life. How grateful I am for Your unfailing love. Each day I find refuge in the safekeeping of Your protecting wings.

Whenever I come to You, I feast on Your Word and drink from Your rivers of cleansing delight. I praise You, Lord, for You are my living Fountain, giving me abundant life.

I Will Follow You

Show me the ways You want me to go, O Lord. Keep my paths right and true. Guide me with Your truth and righteousness.

When I mess up, thank You for being here and helping me back to the right path. I will follow You all my life and bless Your name forever.

Where He Leads Me

I can hear my Savior calling,
I can hear my Savior calling,
I can hear my Savior calling,
"Take thy cross and follow, follow Me."

Where He leads me, I will follow,
Where He leads me, I will follow,
Where He leads me, I will follow;
I'll go with Him, with Him, all the way.

ERNEST W. BLANDY, 1890

Chapter 10

THANK YOU FOR TRIALS

God is our refuge and strength,
an ever-present help in trouble.
Therefore we will not fear,
though the earth give way
and the mountains fall into the heart of
*   the sea,*
though its waters roar and foam
and the mountains quake with their surging.
Selah

PSALM 46:1–3 NIV

But as for me,
I trust in You, O LORD;
I say, "You are my God."
My times are in Your hand.

PSALM 31:14–15 NKJV

DEPRESSION

My nights are sleepless again, dear Lord. Shadows creep around my room. I toss and turn in anguish. When I finally do sleep, I bolt up in bed, frightened that something or someone is after me.

I realize I need Your help more than ever. Life is too tough for me to handle. Lead me to people who can help. Open my mind to ways for me to overcome this terrible depression.

At times, I am so distraught I can't even pray. Yet Your Holy Spirit knows my heart. I know You are lifting my needs to my heavenly Father in words that can never be expressed by any human. I take comfort in that.

Let me give my burdens all to You, my Lord. I must let You carry them for me. Most of all, help me be willing not to take them back.

I know You watch over me and will help me through this. I put my trust in You. I won't depend on my own understanding. I purpose to acknowledge You in every way and to be alert to Your direction. Let me not worry. Help me do my best to solve each problem as it comes along and pray about everything, large and small. Here are my anxieties and my problems. I thank You for Your answers, given according to Your will. You know my needs before I ask.

In doing this, I pray that You grant me peace of heart beyond my comprehension. (Peace is not the absence of problems but a new perspective from You for my life.) Guard my mind and soul against all that isn't honorable to You or best for my well-being.

Finally, dear Lord, enable me to fix my thoughts on You and things that are positive, true, and worthy of praise. No matter what kind of circumstances I am in, let me be content in Your leading. Whether I am well-fed or hungry, in plenty or want, healthy or ill, I know You will guide me through by Your strength.

Thank You, Lord, for Your love and peace. Thank You that You will meet my needs.

I love You, in Jesus' name, amen.

AND CAN IT BE THAT I SHOULD GAIN?

Long my imprisoned spirit lay,
Fast bound in sin and nature's night;
Thine eye diffused a quickening ray—
I woke, the dungeon flamed with light;
My chains fell off, my heart was free,
I rose, went forth, and followed Thee.

CHARLES WESLEY, 1738

PUSHING OUT THE CLOUDS

Do you ever feel overwhelmed by circumstances you can no longer handle? Are anxiety and despondency flooding over you to the point where you can't sleep, and when you do, sleep comes at the wrong times? Perhaps terrible nightmares even bolt you out of bed. Do little things become huge? Are you fearful? Do you want to give up? At times, this can be a simple case of the blues. The blues can grow darker, however, and develop into depression.

We must remember how God is far greater than the most serious of our problems. He is the master healer of our bodies, emotions, and souls. God tells us to take our burdens to Him. He helps make things easier and lightens our loads when we trust in Him. Moreover, He provides us with Christian pastors, counselors, doctors, loved ones, and good friends. Don't be afraid to lean on Him and those who love you. You don't have to go through it all on your own.

God loves you. He cares, even when you are at your lowest ebb. He is your retreat, your security, and your strength. He is *always* present—in the good *and* bad. Through His power, God is calling you to push out the clouds and see clear blue skies and bright yellow sunrises. As we turn to Him, He guides us into joy and peace and hope for the future.

Blessings in Disaster

Dear Father, this awful thing that has happened is shocking. Although I'm in a fog, I feel You carrying me already. Thank You for doing so.

I'm not at all courageous on my own, Lord, but I know You are on my right and left. You go before and behind me as I struggle to get through. Thank You for sending me people who help. I praise You for Your love and care and for never leaving nor forsaking me.

And we know that in all things God works for the good of those who love him, who have been called according to his purpose.

Romans 8:28 niv

My Battles Belong to You

Father God, this looks like it will be a challenging day, but I still must put forth my best for You. I don't know what will happen, so I turn to You for guidance and help. Grant me strength and wisdom to do and say what is acceptable in Your sight.

Thank You for giving me stamina through Your mighty power. I read Your Word and feel dressed in Your sturdy armor—not as a gimmick but by obeying the lessons You teach me in Your Word.

I'm grateful that the spiritual battles I face are not mine. They are Yours, Lord God—battles between You and the evil one. No matter the circumstances, I will not shrink in fear. I shall not despair and faint. For You are with me, ready to fight in my stead.

Help me not to crumble under the circumstances but to triumph over them. Grant me the endurance to stand firm for what is pure and right in Your eyes.

I place my hurts and fears, my actions and attitudes in Your hands. I lift my petitions to You in prayer. I trust You to manage each one according to Your will. Lord, I thank You and praise You already for answers to prayers and victories to come!

Someday, Lord, I want to be able to say like Paul, "I have fought the good fight, I have finished the race, I have kept the faith. Now there is in store for me the crown of righteousness, which the Lord, the righteous Judge, will award to me on that day—and not only to me, but also to all who have longed for his appearing" (2 TIMOTHY 4:7–8 NIV).

BE STRONG IN THE LORD

"Be strong in the Lord
And the power of His might!"
For His promises shall never, never fail;
He will hold thy right hand,
while battling for the right.
Trusting Him, thou shalt forevermore prevail.

EL NATHAN, LATE 1800S

CATHY'S STORY*

For years, Kent and Cathy Shoop loved singing about God's love in churches and meeting places throughout the country. Kent belted out a clear tenor, and Cathy's soprano voice sounded like a bird set free.

A few years ago, God called the couple to pastor a church in Tacoma, Washington, about ninety miles from their home in Easton. Cathy worked as librarian and student activities advisor for a local school district, and they both loved their home nestled among the Cascade Mountain trees, so they decided to commute each weekend to the church congregation they also loved.

Each Friday night, they packed and drove over the pass to their small apartment in Tacoma, where they held worship services, visited people, and entertained company. On Sunday afternoons, they returned home to the weekly work routine. Kent and Cathy continued singing in churches and at special events. Kent accepted a position as chairman of all the denomination's Pacific Northwest churches. Filled with ambition, they loved being active.

One Tuesday morning in early November, Cathy dressed in full winter gear, including mittens and hat, and started out for an aerobics class at Roslyn Fitness Factory ten minutes from home. She would arrive by six thirty, work out, shower, and return to Easton in time for her workday.

Without warning, Cathy hit some black ice on Bullfrog Bridge. The car went into a spin and struck the right railing. Then it pitched into the air and flew over the side, landing upside down on the riverbank below.

Cathy found herself sprawled flat on the ground near her crushed car. She wondered why she couldn't move. She didn't feel cold, but she attributed it to her warm clothing.

Cathy drifted in and out of consciousness. She wondered if anyone could see her below the bridge. Kent wouldn't even miss her for an hour, when she was due at school. Indescribable peace came over her. She felt completely removed from everything. As she lay on the bank, God's presence and glory filled and surrounded her. Cathy knew God was in control.

Forty-five minutes dragged by. A screech of tires and a crash rallied Cathy as another car spun out and lodged itself against the bridge's railing. Cathy heard another car pull up. Two doors slammed. People were talking! Cathy mustered all the strength she could and cried for help. Thank God, they heard her. Immediately, someone called for an ambulance on a cell phone.

Cathy learned later that Kent received a phone call from her school asking why she hadn't shown up for work. He left immediately, retracing Cathy's driving route. By the time he reached the bridge, she had already been transported to the emergency room. How frightening it must have been for him to see the demolished car!

The first thing Cathy saw when she came to in the emergency room was Kent's loving face, filled with fear and concern. Her heart went out to him. "I'm sorry, honey," she stammered. She continued reassuringly, "Kent, don't worry. God is so big and real. God is alive and good!"

Kent told Cathy he had called their grown children. Again, she was sorry. A helicopter emergency crew struggled to keep Cathy alive as they transported her to Seattle's Harborview Medical Center. Cathy had ruptured her spleen, punctured a lung, and suffered a compressed spinal cord. She didn't remember anything from entering the emergency room until after the first week in the hospital, where she teetered between life and death.

When she rallied, Cathy was told she was paralyzed from the chest down. God's presence continued to surround and strengthen her. She never felt angry about what happened.

The scripture "Though He slay me, yet will I trust Him" (Job 13:15 NKJV) gave Cathy courage and strength. A huge drive grew within her to keep going. With her determination and her family's love, she could do it. Most of all, Cathy knew God was helping her. Intense physical therapy began as she pushed herself forward. Her main focus was: "I can do all things through Christ who strengthens me" (Philippians 4:13 NKJV).

Five months after the accident, Cathy returned to school in her wheelchair as librarian and student activities advisor. Kent and Cathy continued pastoring the congregation in Tacoma, driving back and forth each weekend.

Cathy could see Kent's growing fatigue from juggling responsibilities, so she offered to help. She took on the district's bookkeeping job. For three years, Kent and Cathy struggled to carry their load, working night and day. Cathy kept thinking, *"I can do all things. . . ."*

Then she felt her energy level crash. Cathy found herself physically crumbling under the load. The words "I can" were beginning to backfire. God was trying to teach Cathy she could do all things *through Christ* as *He* strengthened her.

After much consideration and prayer, Kent and Cathy felt God leading them to pastor a church closer to home. The district work has now leveled off, and Cathy is learning to pace herself in school, church, and district responsibilities. Hard-learned lessons have taught her to lean more on God. Daily growth in the Lord makes her feel cleansed and complete. Little events and material things are less important. Life and time to accomplish God's will are precious.

Amazingly, Kent and Cathy still give wonderful messages in song, testimony, and example for God.

*Written by permission from
CATHY SHOOP

Lord, Take Me Home

At times like this, Lord, I can hardly stand all the hurts, tragedies, and sin in this world. I'm forced to brush shoulders with it every day.

It grieves me when loved ones and friends fall away from You, marriages dissolve, and disasters strike, over and over. What bothers me most is when I see little children suffer from abuse, illness, and neglect. Lord, please take me home; I'm tired of being here. I feel ashamed to pray this way. But oh, the pain. Thank You for loving me in my weakest moments.

I read in Your Word where You said, "Not My will, but Yours, be done" (Luke 22:42 NKJV). If You need to keep me here, so be it, dear Lord, although I long to be with You. As long as You have a purpose for me, I will serve You with all my heart. Grant me comfort and strength, I pray. And, Father, when You're finished with me here, I'm ready to come home to You.

Strengthen the feeble hands, steady the knees that give way; say to those with fearful hearts, "Be strong, do not fear; your God will come, he will come with vengeance; with divine retribution he will come to save you."

Isaiah 35:3–4 NIV

Chapter 11

THANK YOU FOR BEING NEAR

"Fear not, for I am with you;
Be not dismayed, for I am your God.
I will strengthen you,
Yes, I will help you, I will uphold you with
My righteous right hand."

ISAIAH 41:10 NKJV

As for God, his way is perfect; the word of
the LORD is flawless. He is a shield for all
who take refuge in him. For who is God
besides the LORD?

PSALM 18:30–31 NIV

Your Surprising Presence

I've been so busy today, Lord, going full speed ahead, keeping all my goals in a nice, neat row. Then it happened. Circumstances changed everything.

Thank You, once again, for helping me remember You are really in charge. Thank You for interrupting my busy thoughts and letting me know Your plan.

I never cease to be amazed at the perfect, yet unexplainable, ways You work. How did this happen, Lord? I can't understand it. Thank You for Your surprising presence and Your marvelous ways.

Great is the LORD and most worthy of praise; his greatness no one can fathom.

PSALM 145:3 NIV

The Shelter of Your Presence

In the shelter of Your presence
    You allow my soul to hide.
There You teach me many lessons,
    As You keep me by Your side.

Stress and turmoil won't destroy me,
    Though the storms and tempests come.
I've a shelter in Your presence
    Where You welcome me back home.

PRAISING YOU AT DAWN

I wake in the hush of night with dawn lacing together shadows and shimmers, silhouetted by a silvery moon. I slip outside and listen to the silence. Might I hear Your voice? A cool rush of wind passes through. I see a small wild animal dart from bush to bush, unaware of my presence. I didn't realize such animals were so near. The wind whispers quietly as if to say, "Be still and know God is also near."

A rooster crows from afar, greeting dawn before I even see it. A robin signals to her family from a nearby tree. In wisdom, You so magnificently made it all.

A pale blue glow creeps across the sky, first caressing the trees, then kissing the flowers with tiny drops of dew. *"Savor this moment,"* I feel You say. *"Carry the strength I give into your busy, strenuous day. My Spirit goes with you. Take time today to bless others."*

Ah yes, Lord, I will.

YOU ARE NEAR

When morning skies break and begin a new day,
    You are near.
When I give You my prayer and offer You praise,
    You are near.
When schedules are hectic and stresses are great,
    You are near.
When things don't go right and I ask You for help,
    You are near.
When troubles surround me and all is a loss,
    You are near.
When I do a job well with a feeling of pride,
    You are near.
When loved ones are kind and a child gives a hug,
    You are near.
When I lie down at night and give You my praise,
    You are near.
When sleep overtakes me until the new day,
    You are near.

Protection from Danger

This situation terrified me, Father. I know You must have been with me. Can anything snatch me from You? No. When I was in danger, I thank You for surrounding me within Your protecting arms. You made me alert and gave me wisdom and caution.

I praise You for how Your angels encamped about me once again and delivered me from harm. I wonder what Your angels look like. Do they dress a certain way? Do they draw shining swords and surround me? Or do they look like ordinary people? Because You are my Lord, I shall not fear. You are near, guarding and guiding me all the way. Thank You for never sleeping or turning Your back on me. I will tell everyone I know You are my Savior, my Protector, my Mighty God.

After this moment of danger, I sigh with relief and praise You for taking my hand and leading me to safety.

Your Altar

Here I stand in Your sanctuary, Lord Jesus, hungry, thirsty for Your closeness. The last hymn is being sung. I want to throw myself on Your altar, but what will people think? Will they view me as a troubled, lost soul, or might they grant me those few moments of peace at Your footstool? No one else is up there. Will I disrupt things?

Lord, Your altar is precious to me. I know You are nudging me right now to simply kneel there for a moment, to drink from Your living water and share my thoughts with You. I can't let my pride come before You.

I push one foot forward. As quietly as possible, I slip to one end of Your altar and feel Your overwhelming love and strength. What is that vibration in the floor I feel? Why, here comes another and another to pray.

Thank You for Your nudging Spirit, dear Lord. Thank You for meeting me here, again.

THE TALLEST LADY EVER SEEN

Our six-year-old son, Jonny, had been waiting impatiently for his first bike. Living on a busy street corner delayed his getting one. Plans were already in the works for our family to move to a quieter city and street where it would be safer for him to ride.

We didn't know at the time that Jonny was having repeated dreams about a bike accident. He dreamed he was riding with a friend, whom he had never seen before. It always ended with him flying over the handlebars.

After our move, Jonny got his bike. He was a little shaky but did fairly well on quiet streets. One day, he and his new friend, Mike, rode their bikes halfway around the block to a cul-de-sac. At the time, I was in the kitchen cooking dinner. All of a sudden, I heard Jonny's screams as he approached our front door.

The door flew open, and I heard a lady calmly tell him, "It's all right. You're home now. You're going to be all right."

I rushed to the living room. Jonny was extremely frightened, his face covered with blood. I eased him to the couch and hurried to the door to thank the lady for bringing him home. I glanced up and down the street, but I couldn't see her anywhere.

Jonny sobbed uncontrollably. He shook so hard he couldn't talk. Bob and I hurried him to the hospital emergency room. The nurse wheeled him immediately off for X-rays, while we waited anxiously for Jonny's return.

After he was wheeled back, we gazed at our little boy. Once filled with fun and enthusiasm, Jonny looked tiny and helpless under the cool sheet. Bob and I took his hands and prayed for him to be well and calm. Jonny finally started to relax. He explained that while he and Mike were riding, their bicycle wheels tangled. Jonny lost his balance and flew over the handlebars.

Jonny paused, and a peaceful look came over him. "Mom and Dad, the tallest lady I ever saw came over to me. She was nice and was very strong when she helped me up. She kept talking with me while she walked me home. Mike was so scared that he followed from behind. Then he ran home to his house."

Jonny told us about his dreams. He realized now Mike had been the boy he had dreamed about.

We were thankful when we found out Jonny had only a broken nose and no other serious injuries.

Weeks passed, and Jonny mended nicely. All he could talk about was the nice, tall lady. If she hadn't been there, we wondered if Jonny might have gone into shock.

Jonny rode his bike to the area of the accident in search of the lady to thank her. He knocked on doors, asked neighbors, but couldn't find the lady.

Mike and Jonny never talked about the accident. Mike moved to a different area, and the boys didn't see each other for several years. One day, their paths crossed. In their conversation, Jonny (now Jon) mentioned the bike accident and the tall lady he could never thank.

Mike looked awestruck. "I thought you were talking to yourself. Jon, there was no lady walking you home!"

The boys stood and stared at each other in amazement. Jonny knew the tall lady helped him, and I heard her talking at our front door.

We don't know the answers, but we do know God watched over our six-year-old son that day.

The angel of the LORD encamps around those who fear him, and he delivers them.

PSALM 34:7 NIV

HOLY GROUND

Here I stand, Lord. My kitchen sink may be my only altar, but You are so near to me I can nearly reach out and touch You.

Through the night and early morning, I have sought Your direction. At this moment, You unexpectedly shower me with Your glorious love. Your awesome presence is almost too great to bear. I feel like I should remove my shoes, like Moses did, as though I am standing not on simple tile, but holy ground.

How can You be so wonderful, my Lord? All this time, I have been pleading with You for my needs. You have taken them to Your Father, interceding on my behalf. Thank You.

Just as You prayed in the Garden of Gethsemane before dying for the sins of all humanity, You are taking my needs to the Father right now.

I praise You, Lord, that so many years ago You caused the thick curtain in the temple to rip from top to bottom, exposing the holy of holies to all who love and obey You. No longer are we separated from our Father's presence. Because of this, I can go right in and pour out my soul to You, anytime, anywhere.

Remain with me, I pray. Linger with me just a little longer, so I may bask in Your warm, refreshing presence. Teach me what I must learn, and help me obey. Fill me to overflowing with Your Holy Spirit. Thank You for Your touch, Lord, for letting me stand on holy ground.

PRAISE DESTROYS THE DOUBTS

Father, life is crushing in on me. I can scarcely feel Your presence. My mind whirls with jumbled thoughts: happy, sad, joyous, confused. Do You hear me? How might I feel Your needed presence? I understand You are here, but I don't always take time to heed Your presence. Please help me to do so. Instead of doubting, I will praise You for what You have already done.

Thank You for allowing me at any time, anywhere the privilege of walking into the very holy of holies and communing with You. As we talk and I *listen*, You replace my doubt with Your encouraging presence.

The Roughneck Rooster

If God is for us, who can be against us?

ROMANS 8:31 NKJV

A roughneck rooster, Sasquatch, reigned over my dad's complying hens. The obnoxious, beautiful bird often strutted about, brightly colored feathers on his neck bristling, his tail royally swaying behind him. The comb on his arrogant head and the tip of his curved tail feathers often touched. The rooster had been transported to Washington from Iowa, where farmers had labeled him an exotic bird. Neurotic was more like it! Back and forth he marched, like a grandly decorated army sergeant.

The only persons who could trust the feisty creature were Dad and my daughter-in-law, Stayci. Even the man who delivered the propane oil to Dad's vacation trailer was afraid of the intimidating beast. Yet every time Dad approached Sasquatch, the rooster fluttered to his shoulder and nestled up to him like a dove. Because of his fondness for the watchdog rooster, Dad tolerated Sasquatch's misbehavior. He frequently warned those coming to his home to be on the lookout.

Our two-year-old grandson, Harrison, didn't handle Sasquatch very well. Our son and daughter-in-law lived next door to Dad at the time. Harrison appeared leery of Sasquatch. He watched him with saucer-shaped eyes every time the rooster came in sight. Sasquatch soon picked up on Harrison's fear.

The rooster began chasing him whenever given the chance. Each time, Harrison frantically ran for his front porch, with Sasquatch gleefully padding behind him. The rooster's intimidating feathers rustled, accompanied by brawny squawks and crows.

One day, while Harrison was playing in the yard, out came Sasquatch—neck feathers bristling. Little Harrison determinedly stood his ground. Sasquatch strategically raked his spiky feet in the dirt. Though trembling in his sneakers, Harrison stood tall. The little guy never said a word; he just stared that rooster right in the eye. All of a sudden, the bird slowly turned and sauntered away. Harrison looked surprised at the outcome of this standoff. Sasquatch glanced back one more time. Strangely, the saucy bird was looking past Harrison.

When Harrison turned around, there was big, tall "Chicken Grandpa" (that's what the grandkids call him) standing behind his little great-grandson. Hands on hips, Dad made it clear to the rooster to let his great-grandson be!

Not long after, Sasquatch was traded to another farmer to rule over their chicken flock (and probably the farmer).

Like Harrison, we as Christians face roughneck roosters in our lives. Sometimes they are scary and intimidating. They can even cause us grief.

One thing to remember is we are not alone. Our

heavenly Father is right there with us, fighting our battles when things get a little crazy. We belong to Him, and we are loved with an everlasting love. All we need to do is stick close to God, remain true, and allow Him to help us. When we are mistreated for living Christian lives, we must remember the Lord is our defense. He will remain near and show us a way of escape.

How Close You Are

How close You are, Lord,
    When evening shadows fall.
Streaks of twilight linger;
    then darkness covers all.

How close You are, Lord!
    I hear Your voice so clear.
I feel Your tender touch,
    Your gentle presence near.

Chapter 12

THANK YOU FOR PRAYER

Likewise the Spirit also helps in our weaknesses. For we do not know what we should pray for as we ought, but the Spirit Himself makes intercession for us with groanings which cannot be uttered.

Now He who searches the hearts knows what the mind of the Spirit is, because He makes intercession for the saints according to the will of God.

ROMANS 8:26–27 NKJV

I waited patiently for the LORD; he turned to me and heard my cry. He lifted me out of the slimy pit, out of the mud and mire; he set my feet on a rock and gave me a firm place to stand.

PSALM 40:1–2 NIV

I Will Trust in You

Father, during the past, present, and future of my life, I thank You for helping me be strong and of good courage. I will not fear, for You are the Lord, my God. Thank You for always being with me.

Through the ups and downs in my life, I know You never fail me. Even though I have my own ideas of how my life should go, You know what is best and will always care for me.

Yesterday is past, today is fleeting, and tomorrow is around the bend. Life is too short for me to hold on to any phase of my life and miss out on the blessings You have in store down the road.

Help me forget what is behind me and look forward without fear toward things to come. I will press toward the goals You set for me. Each time I hear You call, I will follow.

Remind me, Lord, to hold on to a positive attitude. Help me focus on whatever is just and pure. Encourage me to think about things that are lovely, honest, and encouraging. Let me look for the best in situations and people, and exercise a positive outlook.

In all circumstances, I will trust in You. Each day, as I follow Your leading, I will build from the past, take advantage of the present, and look forward to the future. Because of Your goodness, I thank You for a peace that surpasses all understanding.

My Own Private Altar

Lord, family strife is crushing in again. I've tried making peace between family members before, but I've found myself caught in the middle. Now, though, I've discovered my own private altar.

Each time the hurt feelings fly, I retreat to that altar and raise our needs to You. A peace settles on our home. You intervene where I can't, and You bring love back where it belongs.

Once again, I retreat from the clamor and bickering. I silently slip through the door. I close and lock it. On my knees by my altar, I lift my heart in praise, urgent petition, and love. Ah yes! I can already hear the peace, and I sense Your work has begun.

Thank You, Lord, for my own private altar. My knees press on hard tile with one little rug. The air is filled with disinfectant. My elbows rest on smooth porcelain. Though my prayer room is my bathroom, my altar my bathtub, at this moment, it is my holy of holies.

My heart rejoices in You. I return to my duties until the next time I come here to meet with You.

You Are My Rock!

Heavenly Father, as I bring my cares to You, I fully trust You to handle them in Your own way. I love You, Lord. You are my rock and my strength. You are my fortress and my rescuer. In You, I will put all my trust.

Each day, I call upon You, who is worthy of my praise. Each day, I need not fear, for I know You battle on my behalf against the forces of such an evil world.

When pangs of illness and death surround me and when torrents of ungodliness assail me, I flee to Your open arms. There, You are ready to hear and help me.

I will trust in You, Lord, rather than my own understanding. In every circumstance, I will acknowledge You. For You, Lord, direct my paths. The joy You give me from Your love is my strength. I thank You and praise You for Your loving-kindness!

In Jesus' name, amen.

S-T-O-P

At times, we feel we have a corner on all our off days, mixed emotions, and concerns in our lives. The wonderful part is how much God understands how we feel. After all, He made us.

He knows us through and through. He cares about every area of our lives and is willing to help and guide when we ask.

Our lives aren't too minute for Him to care, because He loves us more than anyone in this world can possibly love. He's all-knowing, just, and understanding. He sees what is best for us even when we don't recognize the answers ourselves.

The next time an off day hits, remember to S-T-O-P:

Stop and pray.

Tell Him how you feel; then listen to Him.

Open your heart to His presence.

Praise Him for His help and understanding.

Do not be anxious about anything, but in everything, by prayer and petition, with thanksgiving, present your requests to God. And the peace of God, which transcends all understanding, will guard your hearts and your minds in Christ Jesus.

Finally, brothers [and sisters], whatever is true, whatever is noble, whatever is right, whatever is pure, whatever is lovely, whatever is admirable—if anything is excellent or praiseworthy—think about such things. Whatever you have learned or received or heard from me, or seen in me—put it into practice. And the God of peace will be with you.

PHILIPPIANS 4:6–9 NIV

"PRAISE WORKS"

I have a pair of praying hands
A friend once gave to me.
Beside them is the motto:
"Praise works," for all to see.

When I am gazing at those hands,
I think of all You've done.
I lift my praise with grateful heart,
And You and I are one.

"Praise works," I hear You telling me
As I dress for the day.
Each duty, You will guide me through;
Each toil, You'll show the way.

I do not know what each day holds,
I do know One who's there.
No matter what, I'll still recall,
"Praise works," in simple prayer.

Stress and pressures still will come,
With weight beyond degree.
Yet I will keep my thoughts on You,
And praises lift to Thee.

When I begin my projects,
My motto shines out clear:
"Praise works." You whisper tenderly,
"My strength for you is here."

As I'm about to leave my home
To face another day,
"Praise works," I hear You say again.
I pause. I kneel. I pray.

In those kneeling moments,
I lift my praise once more.
I give You my decisions,
And *then* step through the door.

Returning at the end of day,
I think of praise again.
I thank You for the things You've done,
My Savior and my Friend.

I Will Wait on You

Lord Jesus, I wait for You to answer my prayer. The time seems an eternity. I love You and strive to do Your will. Must it take so long?

Grant me patience, I pray, for I realize Your timing and wisdom are perfect. You know my prayer before I ask. I believe You have already brought it to Your Father in heaven on my behalf.

I trust You and will not fear as You determine the best way to answer my prayer. I leave my request at Your feet and will rest in Your constant love and care.

Thank You for Answered Prayer

Thank You again, dear Father, for how You wondrously answered our urgent prayers. They were so personal we couldn't bring them to a large group of believers. Although our numbers were small, we thank You for being with us.

Thank You for how You directed us and performed Your miraculous will to meet our needs. We praise You for Your wise and perfect plans and the way You surrounded us during this time with Your unwavering love and presence. When we became anxious and wanted to take back the burdens, You reminded us to leave them with You.

Thank You for Your comforting Holy Spirit, even when there were only two or three of us praying. Because of Your faithful love and care, we will praise Your name forever.

C. J. AND THE CAT

Ten-year-old C. J. had been in my Sunday school class for two years. I knew him well. One Sunday morning, he shared a prayer request with us. He wanted prayer for his sick cat. I lightheartedly added the request to several others as we prayed.

The next Sunday, C. J. told how his cat was getting worse and the veterinarian was concerned about the cat's recovery. It came time for morning worship service. When my husband, Bob, asked for prayer requests, C. J. raised his hand and asked for prayer for his cat.

Bob looked surprised. Some people smiled. Others stifled chuckles. Bob gingerly added C. J.'s request to several others, asking that God would be with C. J.

After church, C. J. came to me. "I want us to pray for my cat, not *me*," he announced.

At that moment, God spoke to my heart. The two of us sat in the back pew in the sanctuary and prayed earnestly for God to heal C. J.'s cat. Then I turned to my dear student and told him to tell everyone he had prayed for his cat and to give God the praise.

What am I saying? I wondered. *Lord, this is really putting our prayers to the test.*

The next week in Sunday school class, C. J. said the cat was recovering. Our class thanked God together.

Later that day, I praised God again for the unexpected little blessing of C. J. and his cat.

Two Mothers, One Prayer

The phone rattled a long, startling ring. Laverne bolted from a restless nap on the couch and stared at the still-cradled receiver. Would this be another prank call or a long-awaited answer?

Laverne and John's fifteen-year-old daughter, Chelsie, had disappeared two months before. She had seemed happy, active in school, sports, and church. However, her parents sensed something was wrong. Chelsie wouldn't talk with them about her problems. What was happening?

Laverne cautiously answered the phone. Wrong number. Or was it? There was a long pause with no voice, then a *click*. Laverne shuddered and replaced the receiver. She threw herself on the couch and sobbed uncontrollably.

"Oh, Chelsie, Chelsie," she cried into the pillow. "I don't even know if you're alive."

Laverne and John tapped every resource they could think of to locate their beloved daughter: police, the news media, posters, letters. Most important, they asked friends and family to pray. Laverne especially coveted the prayers of her dear friend Jennifer.

Exhausted now, paperwork lying by her side, Laverne finally stretched out on the couch and rested. Her thoughts turned to the Lord as she began to pray. "Father," she sobbed through clenched teeth, "I've prayed constantly for help. I still haven't received an answer. Lord, *please* hear our prayers."

More tears spilled, but now Laverne felt the sweet presence of the Lord. She remembered her last conversation with Jennifer. Jennifer's son, Adam, had disappeared four years earlier, when he was eighteen. Jennifer didn't even know if Adam was still alive. Would it be the same with Chelsie?

God helped Laverne recall what Jennifer had said: "A prayer pact is formed between us for our kids, Laverne, so don't fear. God knows the needs of both of them. Let's trust and thank Him daily for answers and help to come."

God's presence grew stronger. Laverne began to pray again. This time, she lifted her heart and hands in praise to God for the answers to Jennifer's and her prayers. An indescribable strength filled her entire being. She felt as though God carried her above the worries and problems, as though He was seeing her through her uncertainties and fear.

Two weeks passed. Each time Laverne felt anxious, she closed her eyes and imagined herself lifting her daughter up and giving her to God. She quoted promise after promise from her Bible of how God cares. She thanked and praised Him repeatedly for His love and compassion.

One evening, the phone rang. A timid voice came over the line. "Mom? Mommy? I want to come home."

After a long talk with her cherished daughter, Laverne hung up the phone, overjoyed. The first thing she did was praise God for answered prayer. Then she called her husband, John, and her friend Jennifer.

Laverne and John's friends and family joined them in giving thanks for answered prayer. Jennifer was especially happy. One of their prayed-for children had returned home safely. Laverne and Jennifer kept trusting and praising God now more than ever for His help in finding Adam.

Adam had been a model child. But in his senior year, he began running with a drinking crowd. One thing led to another. Soon Adam slipped into alcoholism. Rather than bringing shame to his family, he left home, planning never to return.

After four years, Adam ended up on the streets of Los Angeles. Alcohol and drugs had consumed his life. His six-foot-three frame dwindled to skin draped over bones. Each day, he became weaker, sleeping wherever he could. People stepped over and around him on the busy streets, obviously fearful of going too close or getting involved. Little by little, Adam became almost too weak to breathe. He tried to move but could find no more strength.

Far away, Jennifer and Laverne prayed more intensely than ever and offered praise to God for His coming help. Powerful prayers skyrocketed across the country. Mark, a dedicated street minister, spotted Adam huddled and shaking in a downtown unused doorway. God spoke to Mark's heart and urged him to do something. Mark quickly reached down and gathered the foul-smelling, dying young man in his strong arms and carried him to a nearby mission.

Medical help rapidly kicked in. The ID Adam carried provided Jennifer's phone number. She was called immediately, informed of her son's location, and told he might be dying. Mother and son were reunited in a Los Angeles hospital.

Eventually, Adam successfully completed a drug/alcohol treatment program with much prayer backing him up. Chelsie renewed her commitment to God and is now happily married. Adam returned home. He is successfully employed and helps his mother with expenses and maintenance on their home.

Laverne and Jennifer look back and often thank God for answered prayers and continuing new victories.

JOINING HANDS IN PRAYER

How routine it is, dear Lord, for our family to join hands and pray each morning. We ask for Your guidance and protection from iniquity and harm until we return home.

At day's end, I often look back in awe at how You repeatedly honor our brief yet sincere prayers. I scurry through my duties, striving to meet time limits. I may forget how we prayed that morning until the blessings ring through loud and clear.

Forgive me, Lord, for my impatience. I'm forced to work overtime. The car stalls. I hit every stoplight. My knuckles turn white, gripping the steering wheel. The line is long at the store. Still You are with me.

I don't see all the puzzle pieces; I don't always realize how frequently You intervene and protect. Your miracles must be more than I can number.

Thank You, Lord, for watching over us and bringing each of us home safely, all in answer to our routine morning prayers.

Chapter 13

THANK YOU FOR COMFORTING ME

"Blessed are those who mourn, for they will be comforted."

Matthew 5:4 NIV

But You, O LORD, are a shield for me,
My glory and the One who lifts up my head.
I cried to the LORD with my voice,
And He heard me from His holy hill.
I lay down and slept;
I awoke, for the LORD sustained me.
I will not be afraid of ten thousands of people
Who have set themselves against me all around.

Psalm 3:3–6 NKJV

Fill My Cup, Dear Lord

In this quiet hour, I sit and talk with You, my Lord, about all the things in my life. You listen and love and care.

I seek guidance in Your Word as I prepare to embark on a new day. Fill my cup, dear Lord. Overflow my soul with Your warm, loving Spirit. Thank You for soothing and nourishing my thirsty soul.

What God Hath Promised

God hath not promised smooth roads and wide,
Swift, easy travel, needing no guide;
Never a mountain rocky and steep,
Never a river turbid and deep.

But God hath promised strength for the day,
Rest for the labor, light for the way,
Grace for the trials, help from above,
Unfailing sympathy, undying love.

ANNIE JOHNSON FLINT, 1919

God's Calming Way

When the trials, temptations, uncertainties, and anxieties of this fast-paced society beat around us like a one-hundred-mile-an-hour hurricane, we can cling to the solid Rock, Jesus Christ.

There is something about the way He pulls us into the eye of the storm, where we are forced to sit still, listen, and feel His calming presence.

I can't understand how He does it. He just has a way of surrounding us with peace when we stop what we're frantically doing and cry, "Here, Lord, is all my stress, my crazy schedule, my temptations, and my worries. Please help me."

We hand it all over like a desperate office manager does with his or her secretary, and we anxiously wait for everything to be sorted out and put in the right order. Afterward, we sigh with relief and are grateful.

Life's hardships are far more important than a stack of papers. The Savior, of course, is far greater than one efficient secretary. He *is* order and wisdom. He is all-knowing.

Best of all is the peace and calm that follow after we release everything and let God take control with His calming, guiding touch.

In the shelter of your presence you hide them.

Psalm 31:20 niv

Rolling over the Stress

Father, thank You for encouraging me to let go of things. I will, instead, trust You to handle these problems.

Each time I'm tempted to take on more than I should, I pray that You will help me gain new perspective about what is really important in my life. When the pressures come and I have done all I should do, let me roll over my worries and place them in Your faithful hands. Thank You for replacing the stress in my life with security in You.

O Perfect Love

Grant them the joy which brightens earthly sorrow;
Grant them the peace which calms all earthly
    strife,
And to life's day the glorious unknown morrow
That dawns upon eternal love and life.

DOROTHY BLOMFIELD GURNEY, 1883

RETURN TO ME YOUR
GLADNESS AND JOY

My heart faints from all my grief, O Lord. How can I endure much more? Be merciful to me, I pray, and comfort me in my sorrows. My whole being is filled with agony, my soul overcome with distress.

I try everything to get past these sorrows, but nothing works. The comfort from those who care means so much—but it doesn't take away the pain. When I kept silent, my grief worsened. Day and night, I cannot sleep. My strength is almost gone. I turn to You, Lord, and ask for You to deliver me. You are my Comforter, my Guide, my Healer. Return to me Your gladness and joy, Lord, as I put my trust in You. I praise You, my Lord, for walking this road of grief with me. Even when I feel alone, I know You are still here. Your hand lifts me up as You gently lead me through. Your healing balm soothes my soul. Your counsel and wisdom guide me.

Thank You for helping me see beyond the darkness and into the light. You give me hope for the present and vision for the future. Thank You for directing me to let go of the past and move forward with You. With joy and gladness, I praise You for all You do.

Worthiness from Jesus*

Final arrangements were made for Charlene's tragic, unwanted divorce. After her meeting in the lawyer's office, realization hit her with a devastating blow. She reeled from emotional pain as she drove her daughter, Jessie, to a routine eye doctor's appointment.

"Jessie, I'll sign in at the desk and wait for you in the car." Charlene felt like her words weren't even coming from her mouth but from somewhere in the air. Jessie hugged her mom, silently left the car, and entered the office. Charlene leaned her head against the car window and closed her eyes. Gloomy thoughts filled her mind. It must all be her fault. She felt she wasn't worthy of love, not from her husband, not from her children, not even from God. How could she be worth anything to anyone?

A holy presence jerked Charlene out of her ruinous stupor. She realized these degrading thoughts were not of God. He loved her. She was His child.

She sat up straight and began to cry out to God. She didn't care if anyone near her car heard what she had to say. "Lord Jesus," she prayed haltingly, "take control of my mind and emotions. I don't want to be destroyed by all these terrible thoughts. They are not of You."

She prayed for a long time, asking for God's forgiveness and help. She sought help to forgive and prayed for God to guide and encourage her husband, though he loved her no more.

Charlene felt God's presence surround her like a soft, warm breeze. She looked out her front car window and noticed a huge cedar tree towering proudly above the doctor's office. Its strong branches spread protectively over its surroundings.

"Jesus, that tree has weathered all kinds of storms." Charlene's voice lowered to a whisper. "Here it is, firmly rooted in the center of the city. Trees around it have been cut down. It's a survivor.

"I want to be like that, Lord. I have my roots sunk deeply in You. I know You are supporting me. I can stand tall in the midst of what my children and I are going through.

"I feel rejected and unloved right now. Still, I know You love me and are helping me overcome my distress. With You near, I'll grow stronger every day.

"Grant me strength to stand tall like this cedar tree. Give me enough wisdom and grace to be a blessing to those I love."

An amazing peace enveloped Charlene. She rediscovered the unconditional love and understanding Jesus had for her. Because of God's forgiving mercy, she was worthy of His love, and she knew He would lead her through.

*Names have been changed for privacy.
Written by permission from "CHARLENE."

Comforting Arms

Work on my busy night shift came to an end. I bid everyone a good night and glanced at the clock on the way out the door. Almost one o'clock in the morning. Going home at last.

My muscles stiffened as I folded into my Toyota. "Thank You, Lord, for my little car," I whispered.

In only a few minutes, I approached the turn to our house. Lights were flashing everywhere from a police roadblock. There must have been six patrol cars surrounding the area, while a group of people stood on the corner watching.

I made a U-turn and circled the block to reach our home. Two more police cars were parked on the corner near our house. My mind raced, and I whispered another prayer, "Lord, could it be an accident? Is anyone I know involved? I hope everyone is all right. Please help them."

While the questions flew through my mind, my curiosity overtook common sense. The corner was only two houses away; the obstruction, one block down near the apartments, was directly behind our backyard. I decided to walk down and peek around the corner. I would lock my car when I returned.

I was used to coming home from work in the middle of the night. My drives home were always cautious but with almost no fear. "I can't believe I'm doing this," I mumbled. I ventured to the corner house, preparing to take a look, when a *pop, pop, pop, pop* filled my ears. It sounded like gunshots!

I never knew I could run so fast. I flew to my little unlocked car, scrambled in, slammed the lock down, and scrunched as low as I could. My heart was pounding. I wanted to be invisible. Why did the porch light have to be on? (Bless my husband's heart.) And why did it take thirty seconds for the dome light to turn off in the car *after* the door was closed?

I waited until the shots stopped and then slipped out and locked my car as quietly as possible. I fumbled for the house key and entered our welcoming home. Curiosity spurred me on again, so I crept to our kitchen window, overlooking our backyard. *Pop, pop, pop!* The shots seemed closer. This was too scary for me. I hustled down the hall to the bedroom and my sleeping husband.

Pop, pop, pop, pop! The sound rang over our back fence. Fear penetrated my whole being. How far could bullets fly?

Bob rose up in bed. "What was that?" he asked foggily. Bob could sleep through an earthquake.

"It's gunshots!" I whispered hoarsely. "Hit the deck! Keep your head down!" I dropped my purse and bag to the floor. With one great lunge, I dove for the bed and landed with a belly flop, hoping I'd miss Bob in the final *thud*.

"Dear God," I managed, "please help those people out there. Keep them safe." I clung to Bob and shivered with fright. He pulled the covers over me and wrapped me in his arms.

The shots lessened. Bob's breathing slowed to a

steady rhythm. How could he sleep at a time like this? I lay under the covers, shoes and all, for at least an hour, huddled in Bob's arms. My shivering stopped. I waited and listened.

Silence. After a long while, I rose and tiptoed to the window again. I could still see flashing lights. They would be there for a long time. I felt God urging me to trust Him and let those in charge do the worrying. I finally listened to Him and felt a sense of relief as He calmed my fears. I prepared for bed and rested soundly, thankful for God, the police, and the sweet husband I love.

The next day, the neighbors buzzed, although some hadn't even heard the commotion. The police had been called to a domestic dispute. The woman and her children were coaxed from the home, while neighbors were evacuated. The violent man remained inside, refusing to leave. Unsure if he was armed, the police shot tear gas into the apartment. That's what the popping noise was. (It certainly sounded like a lot of gunshots to me.) I thanked God for my answered prayer. No one was harmed.

How many times do we find ourselves full of fear, perhaps with good reason? Fear of danger, bad influences on our children, the unknown, the future. . . The list goes on.

Sometimes, when all is going smoothly, we find ourselves saying, "This is too good to be true. What will happen next? What if. . . ? What if. . . ?"

We have a loving heavenly Father who knows the future and cares for us. We have no guarantees about what will happen, but we do know He loves and watches out for us.

Like Bob did for me that frightening night, God envelops us in His big, strong arms where we'll be safe. He loves us and surrounds us with His protection. He wants our trust in Him in return. Instead of worrying and being afraid, He asks us to leave it with Him and those He assigns to help.

When we cling to Him, His comfort and assurance drive away our fears. Finally, through His tender coaxing, we rest and trust in Him.

Safe in the Arms of Jesus

Safe in the arms of Jesus,
    safe on His gentle breast,
There by His love o'ershaded,
    sweetly my soul shall rest.

Frances Jane (Fanny) Crosby, 1868

Comforter

When Jesus bid His friends farewell,
    He promised peace would remain.
The Holy Spirit came to earth,
    The Comforter is His name.

"And surely I am with you always, to the very end of the age."

Matthew 28:20 niv

Chapter 14

THANK YOU FOR HEALING ME

*Then the LORD. . .said to him. . . . "If My
people who are called by My name will
humble themselves, and pray and seek My
face, and turn from their wicked ways,
then I will hear from heaven, and will
forgive their sin and heal their land."*

2 CHRONICLES 7:12, 14 NKJV

*Who Himself [Jesus] bore our sins in His
own body on the tree, that we, having died
to sins, might live for righteousness—by
whose stripes you were healed.*

1 PETER 2:24 NKJV

THE POWER OF GOD'S LOVE

A cruel scar showed on a nearby tree,
    Fallen branches from storm and ice.
Its trunk was bare along one side,
    Gashed where branches were sliced.

Slow years slipped over the emerald pine,
    Fresh growth began to sprout once more.
New branches, the tree triumphantly raised,
    Far more lovely than ever before.

Each deep scar tells of battles won,
    The tree is changed forever by pain.
Its beauty is filled with character,
    Lessons in healing remain.

A cruel scar showed on a fallen soul,
    Broken feelings from ice and storm,
A heart was breaking deep inside,
    A trembling life, beaten, torn.

Years slipped by. God tenderly touched
    And healed the broken heart once more.
He made the soul both strong and sure,
    Far more lovely than ever before.

Each cruel scar tells of battles won.
    The soul will never be the same.
God brought needed character,
    To praise and glorify His name.

*And the God of all grace, who called you
to his eternal glory in Christ, after you
have suffered a little while, will himself
restore you and make you strong, firm and
steadfast.*

1 PETER 5:10 NIV

FINDING PEACE

From birth, Sandra had been repeatedly abused. No one else knew about it. Physical and emotional hurt became almost unbearable. God helped her. He provided friends who led Sandra to accept Christ as her Savior. Teachers, even strangers, watered the seed of salvation as she grew up.

After high school, Sandra moved away but couldn't be free from hurt and anger. God helped her again.

One Sunday, she went to a nearby church. The people showed her the love she so desperately needed. Sandra's new pastor and his wife spent hours of prayer and Bible study with Sandra, and she learned to give hurts and bitterness to God. In spite of her parents not showing remorse for their actions, she was learning to forgive. Yet the pain remained.

Sandra went with some friends to a women's retreat. Between conferences, she slipped away to a prayer chapel and met with the Lord again. She told Him she couldn't continue with the hurt and grief any longer. In the chapel, Sandra prayed that God would remove it all. He reminded her He was her heavenly Father, that He loved the fragile little girl within her. Then He did something wonderful. Sandra felt like He reached down and wrapped His arms around her, rocking her back and forth while she sobbed out all her bad experiences. She knew He listened and took them all on His shoulders.

Although the past would never be right, Sandra accepted God's comfort and healing. She found peace. When pain and bad memories returned, she gave them back to the Lord, her Healer and heavenly Father.

Hug the Little Girl within Me

Dear Lord, hug the little girl within me—the little girl mistreated and abused. Encircle me with Your everlasting arms. Still my silent sobs. Anoint my head with Your healing oil; free me from nightmares of memories. Touch my scars with Your healing stripes. Soothe each muscle that suffered in anger and pain. I know You suffered, too. Piece together my broken heart. Your heart bled, and You died for me. In sleepless nights, wrap me in Your comforting presence. Let me rest in the shadow of You, the Almighty.

Hug the little girl in me as You cover me with Your feathers like a mother hen does her chicks. I find refuge under Your wings. Help me to face yesterday (wrong as it was), to forgive as You forgive me, and to look toward tomorrow with hope. Your faithfulness will be my shield and rampart. Let me not feel terror by night nor arrows that fly by day. Take my weakness and grant me Your strength. Make my feet swift at the dawning of a new day to do service for You. I go now in praise.

But please, Lord, don't ever stop hugging me.

I bring this condition of mine to You, Lord Jesus. I ask for Your healing presence. I don't know how You will work in my life, but I trust You unconditionally.

Once You prayed in the Garden of Gethsemane for Your Father to take the cup of suffering and death from You. Still, You placed Your love and trust in Him. You asked not for Your will to be done, but Your Father's, instead.

I don't know how or when You will touch me. I only know You are with me, Lord. You supply my needs. You give me peace. You are my peace.

My strength ebbs to near nothing. I feel I can't hold on much longer, but You remind me how in these times You are strong for me.

Let me pour out my troubles to You each day, dear Lord. Others may sometimes tire of hearing my complaints. You, my Lord, always listen, understand, and care. You give me strength for each day.

I know Your healing presence is with me right now. I yield to You, Lord, and give You control of my entire being. Continue to surround me and fill me with Your Holy Spirit. Take this cup from me. Heal me, I pray. In all things, may Your will be done.

I know You love me. I also realize without a doubt You take my needs and concerns to heart, and You want what is best for me.

Thank You, Lord Jesus, for Your healing presence. Because of Your love, let me be a living demonstration of Your power and give You all the praise.

> *Surely he took up our infirmities*
> *and carried our sorrows,*
> *yet we considered him stricken by God,*
> *smitten by him, and afflicted.*
> *But he was pierced for our transgressions,*
> *he was crushed for our iniquities;*
> *the punishment that brought us peace*
> *was upon him,*
> *and by his wounds we are healed.*
> *We all, like sheep, have gone astray,*
> *each of us has turned to his own way;*
> *and the LORD has laid on him*
> *the iniquity of us all.*

ISAIAH 53:4–6 NIV

FREEDOM

Father, thank You for helping me break this terrible habit. It is no longer my habit, because I've given it to You. Thank You for how each time I'm tempted to pick up that crutch again You give me the strength to firmly say, "No!" I'm excited about the freedom You have given me, because I am no longer bound by this awful habit. Thank You for breaking the bonds that once bound me to it. Now I'm filled with joy and gladness in You, Lord Jesus, and have a new, victorious life.

Each day, I commit my life to You. Help me, I pray, to deliberately turn my back on any temptation and not reconsider it. Thank You for giving me strength and victory. I give You all the praise and glory for setting me free!

Have you ever prayed for yourself or someone else to be healed and never expected it to happen? Some may have while praying for Ann.

Ann was pregnant with her third baby. She felt more tired than usual but thought her weariness came from being a busy mother of two growing youngsters. Ann's husband, Bill, worked long hours as a truck driver, so the young mother carried out most household and child-rearing duties.

Ann began feeling intense heartburn and loss of appetite. Her weight suddenly dropped ten pounds, yet she still didn't suspect a problem. The fatigue grew worse. A friend noticed Ann's skin was becoming jaundiced. A trip to the doctor revealed a serious problem. Ann was suffering from severe hepatitis A and B. Being pregnant weakened her body to where she couldn't even lift ten pounds.

Doctors hospitalized Ann immediately. Her husband, children, and friends feared for her life. Ann's family desperately wanted her home and well.

Ann and the doctors were perplexed as to where she had been infected with the terrible disease. The answer never came.

Relatives and friends were alerted to stand by and pray. Ann feared for the well-being of her unborn child and often lay quietly to feel him move. She sensed God's closeness more than ever before in her life.

Days in the hospital bustled with doctors and

nurses. Technicians frequently drew blood. Nights were long. Ann often felt like her blood was racing through her veins. A few times, she almost drifted into unconsciousness, but God's healing presence filled the room and enveloped her in His love. Ann felt it would have been so easy to slip off and go home with the Lord. Each time she began to fade, God brought Bill and her children to mind, and Ann struggled for survival.

The saints continued praying, some expecting a miracle. Strangely enough, one small prayer group considered Ann's condition hopeless. They gave up praying for her, saying she would probably die anyway.

Ann's condition worsened. Her skin turned a bright yellow. She communed with God on a closer level than ever. God showed Ann His plan for her to serve Him. He wanted her to live many more years.

Finally, she made a turn for the better. The doctors informed Ann and Bill that she could return home to her family, but she would carry hepatitis in her bloodstream for the rest of her life. From then on, Ann would have to take good care of herself.

A few months later, she gave birth to a healthy, adorable baby boy. He was born one month early. After that, Ann regained her strength quickly. People referred to them as the miracle mother and baby. The doubting prayer group learned a surprising lesson on faith, miracles, and healing.

Several years later, Ann went into teaching. Twenty years into her teaching career, news came that all educators were being strongly advised to be vaccinated for hepatitis B for their own protection.

Ann informed the school nurse that this was not necessary for her. When she told the nurse she once had hepatitis A and B while being pregnant, the nurse wouldn't believe her and said Ann couldn't have survived something that serious.

To be certain, Ann went to her local doctor for a blood test. It showed her bloodstream was still filled with hepatitis B, even though she was now healthy and strong.

How was this possible? The saints prayed and believed. Ann trusted God and nestled in His healing, loving presence. God had a calling for Ann to touch the lives of countless children.

Ann is still well, teaching and serving God!

In all things, in God's plan, nothing is impossible when we put our trust in Him!

"Who touched me?" Jesus asked. . . .
"Someone touched me; I know that power has gone out from me."
Then the woman, seeing that she could not go unnoticed, came trembling and fell at his feet. In the presence of all the people, she told why she had touched him and how she had been instantly healed. Then he said to her, "Daughter, your faith has healed you. Go in peace."

LUKE 8:45–48 NIV

Healing of the Heart

Misty's stormy years as a teenager had taken their toll. Now twenty-three, she still couldn't get over the stigma of being the "black sheep" in the family. Harsh words and unkind actions by both daughter and parents left scars, threatening never to heal.

Misty had become a Christian and changed her life, but the black-sheep stigma still remained. Each time she saw her parents or talked with them by phone, her hurts returned. Although her mother and father said they loved her and were proud of her, the anger and injured feelings wouldn't leave.

My parents tell me they love me, she pondered. *They say they forgave me for the past. They even ask me to forgive them.* Misty couldn't understand why the pain would not leave.

Finally, she took it to the Lord in serious prayer. She looked up scriptures on God healing those in pain. Misty began praying God would heal her wounds. She asked Him to help her forgive her parents for their unkind words and deeds. Whenever the pain tried to return, she spoke with the Lord and left it with Him.

How could she make everything up to them? Misty would buy them everything in the world, if that would help. God spoke to her again. He touched Misty's wounded soul. He reminded her that her mother and father had already forgiven her. Now God asked Misty to take the final step. She must forgive herself.

Tears flowed. Cleansing confession poured out from Misty to her Savior. She finally turned to her inner self and forgave. The transformation and healing were complete. Misty felt the peace she longed to feel for so long.

From then on, phone calls with Mom and Dad warmed her heart. She really wasn't the black sheep. Instead, she had been the little wounded lamb. Now Jesus, the real Lamb of God, healed her and made her happy and whole.

The next day John saw Jesus coming toward him, and said, "Behold! The Lamb of God who takes away the sin [and pain] of the world!"

JOHN 1:29 NKJV

Your Unfailing Strength

How marvelous and wonderful are the ways You are with me, Lord, giving me daily strength. When I am weak, You are strong. When my faith wavers, You fill me with Your blessed assurance. No matter how gigantic the requests I bring, You handle them, Lord. I stand on Your firm foundation and trust You for strength and healing.

I depend on Your saving grace as I pray for the ones dear to me. Thank You for Your promise to never leave those who trust in You. You are greater than anything I face. I praise You for being my Lord, my God.

He Is Just the Same Today

Is it true that every sickness
May be laid at Jesus' feet?
All my trouble, care, and sorrow,
And I rest in joy complete?

Yes, my brother, in every sadness,
If by faith to Him you pray,
He'll remove with tender mercy,
For He's just the same today.

JACOB W. BYERS, 1897

Chapter 15

THANK YOU FOR REST

But those who wait on the LORD
Shall renew their strength;
They shall mount up with wings like
*   eagles,*
They shall run and not be weary,
They shall walk and not faint.

ISAIAH 40:31 NKJV

"In repentance and rest is your salvation,
in quietness and trust is your strength."

ISAIAH 30:15 NIV

Late-Night Meeting

Late hours and a fast pace frequently made Nancy's profession increasingly stressful and troublesome. This night was more exhausting than most. Nancy glanced at the clock. One hour to go until she could finally return home.

In the back of her mind, she knew where she wanted to be. Nancy looked forward to her time alone with God. Just Him, herself, and the calm.

Nancy wheeled into the driveway. Home at last. Her throbbing feet stumbled to the door. While she turned the key in the lock, Nancy became aware of the silvery moon's reflection. She turned and stared. How it shone in all of its white splendor, as though it was lighting her way.

Nancy crept in silently so she wouldn't wake her family. Her body ached for sleep, but she was too filled with strain to even try. She paused for a moment and listened to the soft, even breathing coming from the bedrooms. Even the dog lay quietly. He knew it was Nancy. No bother.

She sank into a chair near the window and carefully pulled open the curtain. Faint morning shadows played across the yard. By now, the birds twittered from nearby trees. A wild rabbit gingerly bounced from bush to bush. It glanced up at the window, paid Nancy no heed, and went on with its morning rounds.

Silence. Pure tranquility. Nancy pushed the window open and felt the chilly air caress her face. She could feel God's presence as though He had been waiting up for her like a faithful friend.

Little by little, she shared her experiences with God. She complained and worried, laughed and cried, telling Him of each circumstance, asking for guidance. Finally, she thanked Him for carrying her through another night and keeping her safe.

Nancy leaned back and began reading her Bible. She listened while God tended her needs and advised her through His Word.

She brought her family and friends to His late-night throne, thanking and praising Him for past answers to prayers. She placed each of her beloved ones' needs before God and released them to His care.

Her body relaxed; her eyelids grew heavy.

"Rest, my beloved," she felt Him say.

Nancy creaked to her feet, gently closed the window, and shuffled toward a comfortable, welcoming bed.

"Thank You for meeting me here, Lord," she whispered back.

> *"These things I have spoken to you while being present with you. But the Helper, the Holy Spirit, whom the Father will send in My name, He will teach you all things, and bring to your remembrance all things that I said to you. Peace I leave with you, My peace I give to you; not as the world gives do I give to you. Let not your heart be troubled, neither let it be afraid."*

JOHN 14:25–27 NKJV

Getaway with God

Our son and daughter-in-law, Dan and Stayci, live in a quiet area. They are surrounded by a few neighbors with homes nestled between trees overlooking Puget Sound, a Christian camp made for retreats, a bird sanctuary, and a pond.

A pasture and corral housing their horse and goat spread peacefully at the foot of their back upper deck. Even while our grandchildren busily play, the surroundings send out messages of tranquility.

Dan is a morning person like me. He has often told me the most beautiful time of day at their home is when the sun is rising. Peaceful. Birds everywhere. I found myself longing to witness it.

I finally decided to do something about my wish. I asked Dan and Stayci if I could spend the night, so I, too, could take in this beautiful time of day. The answer, of course, was yes.

The time finally arrived. I came home from teaching, packed my bag with odds and ends—the most important being my Bible, notebook, and pen. I gave my husband a good-bye kiss and headed for my adventure.

After a terrific evening together and a quick night's sleep, I awakened at 4:30. I was ready to enjoy a tranquil time with God. I shuffled into the kitchen, attempting not to make a sound.

My nose immediately picked up the warm aroma of freshly brewed coffee Stayci had thoughtfully set the timer for the previous night. I filled my cup and slipped out the dining room door to the deck with my Bible, notebook, pen, and a paper towel in hand.

The full moon cast a silvery sheen upon everything, making the night almost as light as day. Before long, Dan joined me on the deck. He leaned up against the railing, while I relaxed in a deck chair. We were able to have one of those rare times of quiet, sharing our concerns, dreams, and goals over steaming cups.

After a while, Dan went downstairs to his office. Now I was alone with my thoughts—and God.

I spread out my materials and took a deep breath. It was so peaceful. Stars hung lazily in the sky. I felt as though I could raise my hand and take hold of a fistful of the sparkly diamonds. Nothing stirred except the horse and goat, grazing in the pasture. They glanced my way, seeming curious about my intrusion, then returned to munching on grass, quietly standing like statues. I prayed and thought and prayed some more. Sweet-smelling dew settled around me. My mind gradually cleared of the clutter that interfered with my reason for being there. I wiped the dew from the table and materials with my paper towel. I stood, stretched, and slipped inside for a second cup of coffee.

The moon bid adieu and faded. The sun silently crested and painted the eastern horizon with graduated shades of purple, blue, silver, and brilliant yellow. Its rays slivered through the trees of the bird sanctuary across the road, playing hide-and-seek with the shadows.

I took more of my thoughts to God. This time, I was willing to open my heart and listen to what He might be trying to teach me.

"How I long for You to create a clean heart in me, Lord," I whispered. "Teach me from Your Word, I pray. Help me draw from Your wisdom."

The two-way conversation began as I read my Bible. *"Blessed are those who hunger and thirst for righteousness."*

I dried the table one more time and turned to a story in my Bible. I read about a sensitive eight-year-old boy named Josiah, who became king of the Israelites. His life inspired me, the way he did what was right in God's sight.

The rising sun wrapped my shoulders with a blanket of warmth and caressed the muscles on the back of my neck. At the same time, I sensed God's presence wrapping my heart with warm love, security, and peace.

Trees exploded with birds. Hundreds flocked through the air. They soared and dipped in perfect aerodynamic fashion, as though they were performing daily drills. Without hesitation, they followed their leaders—propelling through the air, floating, then gliding to nearby trees and rooftops. Over and over, they repeated their ritual.

Finally, the multitude of fowl settled here and there, finding their morning meals God had provided. Some rustled through bushes and trees, gently chirruping to their young and giving them breakfast. Barn swallows went about their duties to their nested offspring, expertly zooming in and out of the open stable windows and doors, like skillful air force pilots taking off and landing.

How did they become so accomplished? Was it from hours of practice? Could it be by heeding the lessons of those with experience? Or both?

"This is the answer You are trying to show me, Lord," I whispered. "To hunger and thirst for what is pleasing to You. Let me be obedient and glorify You in all areas of my life."

I realized I must search and listen with an open heart. I must follow God's lead and heed the words of wise people. I must apply what I learn to my life and put into practice God's priceless lessons.

I bowed my head, acknowledging the Author of the beauty that surrounded me. My decision-making, goals, wants, and desires were coming into focus, in accordance with His will. At that very moment, I could feel His Spirit fill and nurture my thirsty soul. I knew He was providing me with the righteousness, love, and wisdom I searched for.

Each day, as I return to God and seek His will, I enjoy a fresh, new, strengthening fellowship with Him. Then I am truly blessed.

Power to Serve

Rev. D. L. Moody told of an elderly minister he met who complained of having heart problems. Concerned about his health, the senior minister decided he could preach only once a week. He asked a younger man to do any extra speaking and take over visiting in homes and hospitals.

The older minister heard a short time after about God's anointing power. If only he could preach the gospel just once with the power of the Holy Spirit before he died! He earnestly prayed for God to anoint and fill him.

The next time Moody talked with the minister, the older man's demeanor had completely changed. Empowered by the Holy Spirit, the minister was preaching at least eight times a week and leading people to Christ!

Moody believed most Christian workers do not break down from hard work. Even as machinery breaks without lubrication, Christian leaders give way under the load by working without the ongoing anointing of God's power.

I believe when things get tough, God wants us (no matter how young or old) to wait on Him in sincere prayer until we receive His power from on high.

We can then move forward, not in our own might or will, but by the continual unlimited anointing of strength and direction from God.

"Come to me, all you who are weary and burdened, and I will give you rest."

MATTHEW 11:28 NIV

Thank You for Your Assuring Presence

When I start to worry, I will refocus my thoughts on You, my Lord. Thank You for Your assuring presence, for reminding me of Your loving care. Thank You for being concerned about me.

When I start to agonize about all the things I'm forced to deal with, I look back at what You have done for me. Again, I feel You touch me with a calming assurance. Thank You, Lord, for how You show mercy and help me through when life becomes tough. Thank You for Your assuring presence during serious illnesses and even the death of a loved one. I'm learning not to be troubled about the uncertainties of these big or even little things, nor by what I will eat, drink, or wear. You already know my needs even before I ask.

I have You as my Savior. I'm alive! I will always trust in You.

Instead of worrying about everything, I'm learning to tell You about all that concerns me. Thank You ahead of time for the answers and solutions, because You know what is best for me.

When You search this land for those who trust in You, I pray You will be pleased with a heart like mine.

Now I give You my worries, dear Lord. I find by trusting You, my insecurities and cares are driven away. I have peace that goes beyond all understanding. . .a peace of heart and mind that causes me to rest and be calm within Your assuring ways.

ESCAPING TO GOD

In our busiest and most stressful weeks, some of us take a few moments to daydream about a quiet bubble bath with a good book.

If you had the chance to escape, where would you like to go? The moon or quiet outer space? An airplane ride to watch the sun sink behind the pink cotton-candy clouds? How about a cruise? Hawaii? Deep-sea diving with the dolphins? Relaxing on the beach under the warm sun while waves lap your toes? Floating down a lazy river or riding the exciting rapids? Watching wildlife in a remote field?

I would love to do all these, but one of my favorite time-outs is catching a sunset or sunrise in my own backyard with my husband, my best friend. Years ago, our youngest son, Dave, and I used to camp in the backyard. Staying in the tent wasn't our cup of tea. We loved it under the stars.

We would lie there for hours talking and straining to stay awake, knowing we could see shooting stars from midnight until early morning. Whispering with excitement, we counted them. The next day, we felt refreshed and invigorated by our late-night getaway.

The greatest escapes of all are when we spend time with our dearest friend, the Lord Jesus. He's a wonderful listener. After we talk with Him and wait a little while, He speaks to our hearts and shows us amazing things. We leave feeling refreshed.

Vacations are wonderful, but they are complete when we escape to have time alone with God. No matter where we go, He is there.

The next time you are "getting away," take your Bible so you can find a quiet, pleasant place and enjoy it with the Lord. What a wonderful escape it will be!

CHANGE MY FATIGUE TO FULFILLMENT

Lord, I earnestly seek You in my time of need. I'm tired. My body aches. My soul longs for Your strength and direction. Grant me energy, I pray.

Show me a new lifestyle. Remind me to use Your precepts in all my ways so I don't fret and give up.

Thank You for teaching me how to change my fatigue to energy and fulfillment.

Be at rest once more, O my soul, for the LORD has been good to you.

PSALM 116:7 NIV

BE STILL

"Be still," I hear Him softly say.
"Be still, lay all aside."
He who made the universe stoops down
and gathers up my cares.

"Be still," He chides again.
His work begins within my weary soul.
"Be patient. In quiet stay,
Listen to me."

Though pressed on every side,
I clear my heart and mind.
In timid voice and heart,
I lift to Him my praise.

How quiet, His presence.
How healing, His words.
In hushed awe, I listen.
I savor each one.

My will He bends.
My heart He sweeps clean.
My strength He renews.
My soul He fills to overflowing.

He teaches through His Word.
I heed what He tells me.
I stand and give Him praise.
Together we go forth to serve.

Chapter 16

THANK YOU FOR THE FUTURE

"For I know the plans I have for you,"
declares the LORD, *"plans to prosper you*
and not to harm you, plans to give you
hope and a future. Then you will call upon
me and come and pray to me, and I will
listen to you."

JEREMIAH 29:11–12 NIV

Oh, He has prepared a glorious heaven for you! It is already waiting for you, not merely a throne but steps by which to mount it. Not only a harp but a tune to play on it. Not only a bannered procession but victory which it is to celebrate.

T. DEWITT TALMAGE, 1832–1902

THE FUTURE

Father, thank You for the future. Although there are times I feel unsure about what lies ahead, the future for me and the ones I love is in Your hands. I feel confident You will be with me through the good times and the struggles. While I obey Your Word, You will take my personal concerns to heart and bless me with what You know is best for me.

I will glorify You by committing my future plans to You. For each endeavor, I will trust You to help and direct. As I work within Your will, I know You will bless my labor with success. Thank You for helping me remember to never stray from Your leading. I praise You for strength to do right.

You, Lord, are my Shepherd. How dear You are for providing for my needs, for granting me rest. How marvelous it is when You guide me and give me peace.

I love You for Your kindness and patience with me when I worry about the what-ifs. Your understanding and mercy help melt my fears. Thank You for reminding me often not to worry. Fear does not come from You. I'm in Your hands; You know my needs before I even ask.

Now I take my frustrations and anxious concerns and lay them at Your feet, dear Lord. A huge weight lifts from my shoulders as You pick them up. Thank You for taking them over once again. Through this, I thank You and praise You for all that lies ahead.

I am God, and there is none like me,
declaring the end from the beginning, and
from ancient times the things that are not
yet done, saying, My counsel shall stand,
and I will do all my pleasure.

ISAIAH 46:9–10 KJV

THE SANDS OF TIME ARE SINKING

The sands of time are sinking, the dawn of
    heaven breaks;
The summer morn I've sighed for—the fair,
    sweet morn awakes:
Dark, dark hath been the midnight,
    but dayspring is at hand,
And glory, glory dwelleth in Immanuel's land.

ANNE ROSS CUNDELL COUSIN, 1857

IF YOU SHOULD ROLL OUT THE FUTURE

If You should roll out the future
　　Like a scroll across the sky,
You'd show me stories from days of old,
　　Give guidance none could deny.

If You should reach down Your fingertip
　　And write on parchment for me,
Answers to questions that tear at my heart,
　　And solve all life's mysteries.

Could I fathom the hidden secrets?
　　Would it set my heart at ease?
Or give me burdens far greater
　　And increase my earnest pleas?

You show me in the Bible
　　That although I cannot see,
I have Your presence with me,
　　Now through eternity.

I read the answers You've given,
　　Your promises great and true;
Your fingertip etches deep in my heart:
　　"I'll truly take care of you."

What Is Heaven Like?

What is heaven like? I believe it will be filled with God's enveloping, awesome, unconditional love. A love so perfect no one will hesitate to pass it on to every single soul. There will be no hurt feelings, no skepticism. Each one will love and truly care about everyone else and be showered by God's love.

In this frightening world of violence and disaster, where the poor and uneducated suffer endlessly, our society finds it increasingly difficult to understand and love others. Some, we even fear. We keep trying desperately to find the answers but often come out frustrated.

Sharp, talented, charming, beautiful, and good people are more easily accepted and loved. This is how our world often views things.

God sees it all differently. He cares for the bright, wealthy, and beautiful; He also loves the poor, under-privileged, unattractive, ill-clad, and homeless with an equal, pure love. All of God's children in heaven will be able to love in this way. No more deception. No classes—rich or poor. We'll all be His children—strong, healthy, worshipping God and basking in His awesome presence.

Oh, the joy we'll share as we unite with each other and see our God and His Son face-to-face!

GROWING OLDER

Lord, that big zero in my age just rounded the corner. My friends tease me about being over-the-hill. They say the best of life is gone. When I hear that, I laugh.

I wonder what You have in store for me this next year. How can You use me during this phase of my life? I have no fear of growing older. Life is out there to enjoy. Thank You for giving me one more year to do so.

I will not be poured into an ancient mold. I may be growing older, but I refuse to act old. Old age is an attitude. I'm determined to live life abundantly through Your joy and strength.

I see the trees with their scars and burls. Reflecting Your glorious sunset, their branches reach heavenward and praise You, O God. They have survived many of life's storms, just like me. In the still of evening, I can hear their rustling boughs whisper a night wind's song, thanking You for life.

I'm not ashamed of pain-filled fingers gnarled from arthritis. They show the work I have done for others. I see the wrinkles collecting on my face. Character lines, I call them. I especially like the ones put there from years of smiles. No matter my health, I can always find ways to serve You, such as writing letters to the lonely. Best of all, I can hold others up in faithful prayer.

I thank You, Lord, for life and that You offer it to me in an abundance of spirit and joy. Even when I reach my sunset years, I lift my praise to You. May I reflect Your Holy Spirit all the days of my life.

❦

Jaw set, Orlan bent his head in prayer. His silvery hair

reflected the church sanctuary lights. The ninety-year-old man's eyes shut tightly as he went to war again. Like many other times, Orlan engaged in a spiritual battle through prayer. The need? No matter. Yet one of many answered victoriously.

Orlan's wife, Jessie, sat near him. She squeezed his hand and joined him in prayer. The Holy Spirit surrounded them—perhaps angels hovered, rejoicing, protecting.

Orlan and Jessie have served the Lord most of their lives. They have built churches, taught Sunday school classes, prayed without ceasing, and won souls for Him. Now they move much slower from arthritis, poor eyesight, and dulled hearing. But they keep going and doing for the Lord!

When asked about retirement, they shake their heads and say, "There's too much work to be done." Besides prayer, Orlan is always willing to help wherever possible. Jessie writes cards and notes of cheer. Both willingly lend a hand even when not feeling well.

We must keep using the valuable older people in our churches. They are our cornerstones, our legacies.

They have so much wisdom and experience to offer. Some have given their entire lives for Christ and the church. If they are put on a shelf, their joy in life is snuffed out. God certainly isn't finished with them yet!

As I grow older, I pray I will be allowed to keep a vision, compassion, and dedication so I can serve God with all my strength and being.

Thank you, Orlan, Jessie, and other older folks, for your service and prayers. Keep on keeping on!

Welcome Home

Whenever I think of heaven, a deep, homesick feeling stirs within me. I feel I have been there before my time on this earth began. There is an overpowering love drawing me to run and fall into my heavenly Father's arms.

Like Martha, I want to sit at the feet of my Lord and ask all the questions I've accumulated during my stay on earth. One by one, I believe He'll help me understand the answers.

Perhaps many Christians feel this way who know the Father well. We communicate with Him daily and sense His loving presence. Although I love my husband, family, and friends here, there is a deeper, fuller love I feel for my Father in heaven.

What will heaven be like? The Bible says there will be no more sin or violence, sickness or pain, tears or grief. We often grow weary of fending off these things that cause anguish and stress. We long for a carefree, eternal life with God in heaven. What a delight it will be when we get to see our Christian loved ones and friends who have gone home before us!

But there is more to heaven than this. The glorious, awesome Triune God the Father, God the Son, and God the Holy Spirit is there. Heaven will be more than a blessed revival or camp meeting. We will actually get to meet Him face-to-face!

As I fall before Him in reverence, I can imagine Jesus, my Savior, stepping forward, bending down, and taking my hand. As He helps me to my feet, I may hear Him say, "It's all right, My child. I paid the price for your sins. Welcome home."

> *"Do not let your hearts be troubled. Trust in God; trust also in me. In my Father's house are many rooms; if it were not so, I would have told you. I am going there to prepare a place for you. And if I go and prepare a place for you, I will come back and take you to be with me that you also may be where I am."*

> JOHN 14:1–3 NIV

I Want to Leave My Mark for You

I know not what each day holds or what time I have left to serve. This I do know, dear Lord: I want to leave my mark for You.

Help me make every day count. Remind me to lay aside my own wants, to be willingly inconvenienced and used for You. Let me not put anything before You, no matter how good it seems. Help me shed bad habits that slow me down from doing Your will.

I can only leave my mark for You by replacing idle time with purposeful movement. When I rest, I open my heart, that You may fill me with Your strength and Spirit.

Teach me to let go of yesterday, live fully today, and look with excitement toward tomorrow. I am awed as I daily come to know You more. I feel You shower love upon me like a refreshing summer rain.

Even though I am unworthy, I long to reach the end of life's journey and see You face-to-face. In the meantime, Lord, may I use each day, each hour, each moment to leave my mark for You. Amen.

Heaven

Father, I praise You for the heaven You have prepared for me. I long to see the holy city, to worship in Your tabernacle. It won't be a tabernacle built by hands, but Your enveloping presence, Lord God Almighty, will be the temple.

I don't feel worthy. Thank You for covering me with Your redemptive blood so I may enter.

Will there really be no tears? No sickness? No pain? Will all believers in Christ be alive, happy, and well? Will we never thirst again but drink from the water of life? Ah yes! How grand it will be! Praise You, Lord.

I look forward to entering that holy city, Father. I can't imagine its beauty, the light being as a precious jasper stone, clear as crystal.

You have told me in Your Word there will be no need for a sun to shine by day or a moon by night. For the glory of You, Father, will lighten it, and Your Son, the Lamb of God, will be the light. There will be no need for lights: You will give us all we need. Neither will we have to lock the gates or doors. There shall be nothing to fear.

Best of all, You, Lord God the Father, the Son, and the Holy Spirit, the Alpha and the Omega, the Beginning and the End, shall reign forever and ever!

Beginning a New Life

From the moment we draw our first breath as babies, we have a God-given determination to make these mortal bodies of ours live, grow, and thrive. Life is precious. We want to hang on to it for all we're worth, and we seldom desire to give up this earthly world we know.

When we are about to die, however, I believe God will be with us every step of the way through the valley of death.

It is interesting to note that some refer to the Kidron Valley, located on Jerusalem's northeastern slope, as the valley of death. During winter, Kidron Valley floods with deadly torrents from underground water. In summer, it is dry and unbearably hot. Its steep, naked banks hug dreary burial grounds no one has ever wanted to walk through. When Jesus left Jerusalem on the night of His betrayal, He might have crossed the northern end of the Kidron Valley to reach the Garden of Gethsemane. Those brave enough to walk the twenty miles south to the other end of the valley find the Spring of Gihon filled with pure, sweet water.

When we are about to leave this world and approach the valley of death, we need not fear. Jesus has gone before us. He will be there, ready to take our hands and safely lead us through to His living water and life eternal. These frail bodies we've hung on to so tightly will no longer matter. In light of His glory, we'll shed our mortal shells and realize we aren't dead at all. We shall have new lives that will never end. We won't feel sickness or pain. Sadness and tears will be no more. We shall begin a brand-new life of joy and peace. We will become complete, with indescribable blessings from our Lord.

Talk with Us, Lord

Let this my every hour employ,
Till I Thy glory see;
Enter into my Master's joy,
And find my heaven in Thee.

CHARLES WESLEY, 1740

GOD'S BLESSINGS BE UPON YOU

May you lift your gaze to the heavens
    and hunger for the Lord, your God.
May your help come from Him,
    the Maker of all creation.

May He not let your feet slip
    outside of His Holy ways.
May He keep you safe day and night,
    for He never rests.

May He encompass you
    as you go out and come in.
May the Lord be your shade by day
    so the sun will not harm you.

May He protect you with His mighty hand
    and watch over you—now and forevermore.
Amen.

If you enjoyed

❧ ❧ ❧ ❧ ❧ ❧

THANK
YOU,
LORD

be sure to read these other inspirational
titles from Barbour Publishing.

DAILY LIGHT FROM THE BIBLE
Encouraging Christians for more than two
hundred years, this brand-new edition of the
classic, all-scripture devotional now features a
complete scripture index.
ISBN 1-59310-935-0 / 400 pages / $5.97

DAILY STRENGTH FOR DAILY NEEDS
Bringing classic spiritual writings to the
modern reader's fingertips with 365 daily
readings of prose, poetry, and scripture, *Daily
Strength for Daily Needs* will continue to
enrich generations to come.
ISBN 1-59789-113-4 / 384 pages / $5.97

THE GOLDEN TREASURY
OF BIBLE WISDOM
Offering thoughts on assurance, faith, family,
giving, peace, trusting God, and more, this
modern classic has sold nearly 300,000 copies.
Each brief nugget of truth is accompanied by a
verse from the beloved King James Version.
ISBN 1-59310-934-2 / 416 pages / $5.97

Available wherever books are sold.